Joe Hornby/
A very special
Friend who lives his
in service to others!
God Bless
Joe
3-13-15

WHEN ~~GOD~~ America LEFT ~~AMERICA~~ God

Larry Perry

Performance Press

Chelsea, MI | Nashville, TN | Oak Ridge, TN

Performance Press
PO Box 5194
Oak Ridge TN 37931

Copyright © 2013 by Larry Perry

All rights reserved, including the right to reproduce this book or portions thereof in any form whatsoever.

For information address:
Performance Press Subsidiary Rights Division
Box 5194
Oak Ridge, TN 37830

FIRST PRINTING 4-2013

ISBN: 978-0-942442-40-3

Design by Kim Breasseale
451° Design Studio
Knoxville, TN

Cover painting by
Bobbie Crews
Knoxville, TN

Author email:
larryperry@att.net

Manufactured in the United States of America

Dedicated to Ken Crosthwaite

A true Patriot who pushed and pushed and cajoled me until it was published.

ACKNOWLEDGMENTS

A Special THANK YOU to my wife, Eloise, for her love, support and patience throughout this process. She encouraged and helped with the preparation, editing and typing of the original manuscript.

I want to thank the following for their suggestions, comments, and criticisms throughout the development of this book: Douglas Hubbard, Gloria Epperson, Rita Copenhaver, Eileen Levins, Bird and Michael Minch, Paul Bice, Honorable Don Layton, and those other judges and reviewers who will remain anonymous and who read and helped with the original manuscript.

Also, a big debt of gratitude goes to America's finest Constitutional historian, David Barton, and his team of researchers at Wallbuilders in Texas for their help with the history of the Constitution, and to Kelly Shackelford and his legal team at the Liberty Institute for their research and assistance in the case reviews and who are fierce defenders of Religious Freedom in America.

My heartfelt appreciation and thanks go to the chief researcher for the project, Candyce Leeper of Lincoln Memorial University, whose work and efforts will never be forgotten.

The layout and design work could not have been accomplished without the creative minds of Kim Breasseale of the Design Studio and the cover oil painting by Bobbie Crews.

Lastly, I want to thank those courageous people who have fought to defend our religious freedoms from the onslaught against our religious freedoms in America. We would be a lost cause without you!

TABLE OF CONTENTS

Acknowledgments v

Foreword ix

Introduction xi

CHAPTER 1
THE RELIGIOUS BASIS OF OUR NATION'S CONSTITUTION 1

CHAPTER 2
THE ROLL OF RELIGION IN EDUCATION 17

CHAPTER 3
TIMES ARE CHANGING 29

CHAPTER 4
ATTACKS ON EDUCATION 33

CHAPTER 5
SCHOOL PRAYER 41

CHAPTER 6
TEN COMMANDMENT REMOVAL 57

CHAPTER 7
SCHOLARSHIP/FREEDOM OF SPEECH RESTRICTED IN SCHOOLS 61

CHAPTER 8
ATTACKS ON TEACHERS AND SCHOOL ADMINISTRATORS 69

Chapter 9
Lawsuits Against Churches And Ministries 73

Chapter 10
Religious Group Discrimination 81

Chapter 11
When America Spurned God 87

Chapter 12
The Last Word 93

Chapter 13
Enemies Of The First Amendment 107

Epilogue
Where Do We Go From Here 113

FOREWORD

Did God really Leave America?
Let's understand that **God didn't leave America, America left God! Hopefully, that title got your attention!!!** God is still here for those who believe and trust in Him but reading this book will explain what is happening to our belief system and way of life.

America is a country based on laws which use the Constitution of the United States as a basis and guardian of freedoms and are founded upon Judeo-Christian principles set forth in the Bible and the Torah *(First 5 chapters of the Bible)* as a foundation… a bedrock. The Constitution has survived wars, protests, and legal attacks; but, over the last several decades, the foundations of the Constitution have been put to the test. The moral and religious foundation on which it was erected have been assaulted in the newspapers, on television, and the social networks such as Facebook, Twitter, etc, the courts, and around lunchrooms. They have been called into question with more and more morally aberrant groups proclaiming their right to constitutional protection.

America's founding documents make it clear that the American government must operate according to moral standards set forth by God Himself. In the Declaration of Independence that standard is identified as *"the laws of nature and of nature's God,"* and in our Constitution it is identified as the Common Law which was specifically incorporated into the Constitution through the Seventh Amendment.

The Constitution was not designed to protect individuals from God oriented standards of morality or behavior but, instead, **to protect the nation from court and government sanctioned immorality.** If the foundations of religion and morality are removed from its operations, neither the

Constitution nor the American government will work correctly.

Recently, we have seen children shooting other children in schools, teenaged girls stealing money from Girl Scouts selling cookies, students cheating on college exams, drugs being sold in schools and on the street, politicians passing laws and courts rendering decisions against religious teachings, and other such events. **In short, this country has lost its moral compass….the glue that holds our culture together!**

Why? What has happened to the great country of America to bring us down to this point in from the world's greatest and most blessed, most giving country the world has ever known?

The Founding Fathers considered religious liberty our first freedom and the basis upon which all other freedoms rest. They understood that one's right to worship God and follow His laws and guidance, according to the principles of His teachings, was a fundamental cornerstone to our morality and direction. America today would be unrecognizable to our Founders. The principles and concepts they knew, practiced, and wrote into our founding documents were based on religious freedom, have been, and are being attacked on many fronts by well funded aggressive groups and individuals. They are using the Courts, Congress, federal bureaucracies, and state/local governments to suppress and limit religious freedoms, thus, turning the First Amendment upside down.

The shocking number of court cases, local government rulings, and Acts of Congress which have thrown God out of our daily lives, make it clear that hostility to religion is a very real problem that affects all of us.

In this book, you will see what and why the moral fiber of the country has collapsed and what we have to do to change it.

Larry Perry
Knoxville, TN

INTRODUCTION

America was founded by the early pioneers and early statesmen, on Godly principles such as the Ten Commandments, the Beatitudes, the Golden Rule, etc. The first schools were Christian based schools. The first battles in the new world were based on Freedom of Religion. These Godly principles and guidelines set a moral compass for the people and children of America with things such as, do not kill, do not lie, etc. Now more than 400 years after the first colonists arrived, America has no moral compass.

WHY? What happened to cause this loss of principles upon which this country was founded?

This book will answer these and many other related questions.

Recently, many authors have questioned whether or not the United States of America was founded as a Christian nation. It is interesting to provide a few historical quotes from our Founding Era that lend credence to the position that we indeed were founded as a Christian principle based nation.

In the Declaration of Independence we read, *"When in the Course of human events, it becomes necessary for one people to dissolve the political bands which have connected them with another, and to assume among the powers of the earth, the separate and equal station to which the Laws of Nature and of Nature's* **God** *entitles them . . .*

"We hold these truths to be self-evident, that all men are created equal, that they are endowed by their **Creator** *with certain unalienable Rights . . .*

"And for the support of this Declaration, with a **firm reliance on the protection of Divine Providence,** *We mutually pledge to each other our Lives, our Fortunes, and our sacred Honor."* (emphasis mine.)

Sounds Christian to me!

Now lets talk a little about the Constitution! Granted, "God" is not mentioned in the Constitution but, He is mentioned in every major document leading up to the final wording of the Constitution. For example, Connecticut is still known as the "Constitution State" because its colonial constitution was used as a model for the United States Constitution. Its first words were: "For as much as **it has pleased the almighty God** by the wise disposition of His Divine Providence…".

Most of the fifty-five Founding Fathers who worked on the Constitution were members of orthodox Christian churches, and many were even evangelical Christians as you will see from reading a short history of the country. The first official act of the First Continental Congress was to open in Christian prayer, which ended in these words: "*…the merits of Jesus Christ, Thy Son, our Savior. Amen*". Sounds Christian to me!

Ben Franklin, at the Constitutional Convention, said: "*…**God governs in the affairs of men.** And if a sparrow cannot fall to the ground without His notice, is it probable that an empire can not rise without **His aid?**"* (Emphasis added)

Since the founding of America, the First Amendment to the Constitution has been under attack which is clearly documented in this book.

The intent of the First Amendment, to keep Government from establishing a 'National Denomination' *(like the Church of England)*, was well understood during the founding of our country. As early as 1799 a court declared: **"By our form of government the Christian religion is the established religion** and all sects and denominations of Christians are placed on the same equal footing." Even in the letter that Thomas Jefferson wrote to the Baptists of Danbury Connecticut *(from which we derive the term "separation of Church and State")* he made it quite clear that the wall of separation was to insure that Government would never interfere with religious activities because religious freedom came from God…not from Government. But is that what is happening in America today???

Even George Washington, who presided over their formation, certainly knew the intent of the Constitution and the Bill of Rights. He said in his "Farewell Address": *"Of all the dispositions and habits which lead to political prosperity, **religion and morality are indispensable supports.** In* *vain would that man claim the tribute of patriotism,* **who should labor to subvert these great pillars."** It doesn't sound like Washington was trying to separate religion and politics.

In reading this book, you will be reading many court decisions and will see the impact they have on our lives. This is important to understand the changes we have, and are seeing, in the religious structure and their impact on the morality of our country. This book is not intended to be a textbook for law students but rather a discussion of what is happening to religion in our country, who is causing it and what we can do about it! Most of the cases you will be reading are United States Supreme Court cases with a few from local and state courts that impact what we do and say and how the decisions have attacked the morality of the country.

What does the Constitution say about the courts? Not much. In describing the Federal Judiciary where First Amendment (Freedom of Religion) cases are heard, Article III of the Constitution says, *"The judicial Power of the United States shall be vested in one Supreme Court, and in such inferior Courts as the Congress may from time to time ordain and establish."* Article III also lists several types of jurisdiction that Congress may choose to grant to inferior courts and describes the Supreme Court's original jurisdiction.

In the Judiciary Act of 1789, the first federal Congress established the three-tiered federal court system: (1) A local District Court where federal cases are first heard; (2) A regional Court of Appeals where a case from a District Court may be appealed *(reheard)*; and (3) The United States Supreme Court which has the final say on legal matters. In the judicial system, we have two kinds of courts: courts of general jurisdiction (state courts) and courts of limited jurisdiction (federal courts). Before a federal court involves itself in a conflict, it must decide whether that conflict falls under its constitutional jurisdiction.

Today, the U.S. Supreme Court is made up of 9 members who are appointed by the President and approved by the Senate and who hold that office for a lifetime!!! So, if a President has liberal leanings or conservative leanings, he or she will appoint Supreme Court members who have similar leanings. You will be able to see this in the various court decisions as you read through the cases here. Keep in mind, that a new federal law that is passed by 535 members of Congress *(House of Representatives and the Senate)* and then, signed into law by the President; BUT, it may be overturned by five of the nine people sitting on the Supreme Court. **Now who controls the morality of this country??** *Huh???*

The power and effect of today's Supreme Court would have surprised and horrified the Founders of our country who wanted the individual states to have authority over the citizens of that particular state. However, the US Supreme Court, in a unanimous decision in 1958, denied that state governors and legislators had anything to say about segregated schools![1] It thus declared that it was the decider of all questions constitutional! For example: In state executive and state legislative attempts to circumvent the US Supreme Court decisions, the Court said these were attempts to circumvent the Constitution itself.

Why am I bringing all this up? Because it is important to understand the background and reasoning of many of the court cases you will be reading.

Before we begin, consider the gravity the situation. **Suppose you wanted to take over a country and form it like you think it should be but you wanted to take it over without any military intervention or any shots being fired. How would you do it? Assuming that time was not a problem to accomplish this goal, what would you have to change in the country in order to take it over and in what order?**

The three major things that you would have to destroy are **Patriotism, Morality, and Spirituality.** *But how would you do that? What would it take? How long would it take?* These tactics were and are used by following the Communist manifesto developed by Karl Marx and others and followed by despotic leaders in the world such as Hitler, Mussolini, Lenin and others.[2]

In this book, we shall be talking about how Morality has been essentially destroyed and how Religion is being destroyed in America to achieve what results?

To say that this nation was not founded as a Christian nation or that the Constitution was not founded on Christian principles is totally at odds with the supported historical facts.

Chapter 1

The Religious Basis Of Our Nation's Constitution

In the beginning ...Why must we go back in history in this book? Because most of this basic information isn't taught in public schools anymore and the reader needs this foundation before proceeding with the vital question of what has happened to God in the United States. In order to understand the problems of today, we need to know the origin of our laws.

From the earliest days of American history, the Founders were convinced that the soundest approach to the security and mutual happiness of a nation was to have all the people enter into a solemn agreement with each other reinforced with a covenant (a promise) before God that they would honor their commitments. The earliest, and perhaps the most famous American promise or covenant, was the Mayflower Compact which was signed on November 11, 1620. Under extremely aggravating circumstances, the British settlers were originally supposed to go to Virginia but were blown off course and landed far north of their planned landing site. They sailed on a ship called the Mayflower which anchored in New Plymouth and is currently located near Cape Cod, Massachusetts. This colony would later become the Massachusetts Bay Colony.

Why did they leave England and make their way to the new world? England had decided to separate from the Catholic Church and created the English Church or the Anglican Church. Some of the first settlers wanted to be free to practice their Christian faith the way they wanted to; so, they left and later created the Puritan Church. They were also called Separatists because they separated from the church and even the state. Had they stayed in England, they would either have complied with the teachings of the English Church or they would have been prosecuted and put in prison. Since the settlers did not land in Virginia, but landed outside the area claimed by the English companies, they believed themselves to be independent from any government and decided to create their own colony so that no one would have the power to command them! Later on, the Separatists became known as Pilgrims. Forty one adult males out of the one hundred two settlers on the Mayflower decided to create a law called the Mayflower Compact. They knew that the first group of settlers, those who went to the New World before they did, failed because they did not have any system of self government. To insure their success this time, they decided to create a government; and, the Mayflower Compact was the first law ever enacted in this country. Those who created the Mayflower Compact believed that it was an agreement, much like a promise or a covenant, that was to be honored between God and man and also among all men. It was grounded in faith. In the words of the Mayflower Compact, the purpose of the Compact was to combine themselves into a "civil body politic"…"for the glory of God and the advancement of the Christian faith in honor of their king and country and in the presence of God and another".

In short, they all agreed to comply with their government's laws, and in return, they would all protect one another making it in essence a social contract. According to historians, the Mayflower Compact was the foundation of the United States Constitution, which was written more than 150 years later.

What is the Mayflower Compact?

The Mayflower Compact is a written agreement composed by a consensus of the new settlers arriving at New Plymouth in November 1620 and was drawn up with fair and equal laws for the general good of the settlement and with the will of the majority. The Mayflower passengers knew that the New World's earlier settlers in Virginia had failed due to a lack of a government; so they hashed out the content and eventually composed the Compact for the sake of their own survival.

Being the first written laws for the new land, the Compact determined authority within the settlement and was observed until 1691. This established that the Colony was to be free from English law. It was devised to set up a government from within itself and was written by those to be governed. In creating the Mayflower Compact, the signers believed that the covenants (promises) were not only to be honored between God and man, but also between each other. They had always honored covenants or promises as a part of their righteous integrity and agreed to be bound by the same principle with the Compact.

America was indeed begun by men who honored God and set their founding principles by the words of the Bible. They lived their lives with honesty, reliability and fairness toward establishing this country for the sake of its survival.

The Mayflower Compact was written so that the Pilgrims in America would have laws. They did not settle where the king had wanted them to; so, they concluded that they did not need to follow his laws. They created their own laws.

The Pilgrim leaders realized that they needed a temporary government authority. In England such authority came from the king. Isolated, as they were in America, such authority could only come from the people themselves.

Immediately after agreeing to the Mayflower Compact, the signers elected John Carter (one of the Pilgrim leaders) as governor of their colony. They called the colony Plymouth Plantation. When Governor Carter died, in less than a year, William Bradford, age 31, replaced him. Each year thereafter, the "civil body politic," consisting of all adult males except indentured servants assembled to elect the governor and a small number of assistants. Bradford was reelected 30 times between 1621 and 1656.

In the early years, Governor Bradford pretty much decided how the colony should be run. Few objected to his one man rule. As the Colony's population grew due to immigration, several new towns came into existence. The roving and increasingly scattered population found it difficult to attend the general court. By 1639, the governing meetings at Plymouth were called and deputies were sent to represent each town at the other general court sessions. Not only self rule but representative government had taken root on American soil.

The English Magna Carta, written more than 400 years before the Mayflower Compact, established the principle of the rule of law. In England, this is called the King's Law. The Mayflower Compact continued the idea of law made by the people. This idea lies at the heart of Democracy. From its crude beginning in Plymouth, self government was established and evolved into the town meetings of New England and larger local government in colonial America. By the time of the Constitutional Convention, the Mayflower Compact had nearly been forgotten but the powerful idea of self government had not. Born out of necessity on the Mayflower, the Compact made a significant contribution to the creation of a new democratic nation.

This little vignette from our early history illustrates that the founders had rooted in their souls the firm belief that sound government requires a sacred covenant between the people and themselves. They openly declared this covenant/promise before God as their witness. They were particularly impressed by examples in the Bible where the people prospered both spiritually and mentally, when they had entered a sacred promise with each other before God; so, they made this the foundation of their society.

In fact, they were well aware that the Bible itself is a story of such a promise. The Old Testament was originally called the Book of the Old Covenant and the New Testament was called the Book of the New Covenant. They knew that ancient Israel, as well as the Christians, lost untold blessings because they did not live up to their covenants with God. The most important single lesson to be learned from Old Testament history is that God's law will not function except under the disciplined commitments of a **virtuous people.**

The Founders were well aware that a Constitutional government of freedom, peace and prosperity could only be built within a culture of virtuous and God loving people. Here are some of their statements worth remembering:

Benjamin Franklin said: *"Only a virtuous people are capable of freedom. As nations become corrupt, they have more need of masters."*[3]

John Adams said: *"Our Constitution was made only for a moral and religious people. It is wholly inadequate to the government of any other".*[4]

Samuel Adams said: *"Neither the wisest Constitution nor the wisest laws will secure the liberty and happiness of a people whose manners are universally corrupt".*[5]

One of the problems of the founders was that they were unable to raise up a people sufficiently virtuous and righteous to accommodate the requirements for God's laws. Of course, the same thing was true of Israel. One of the most amazing aspects of the American story is that, while the nation's founders came from widely different backgrounds, their fundamental beliefs were virtually identical. They quarreled bitterly over the most practical plan of implementing these beliefs but rarely, if ever, disputed about their basic convictions or final objectives. Some of these men came from several different churches and others from no church at all. They ranged in occupation from farmers to presidents of universities and their social backgrounds included everything from wilderness pioneering to the aristocracy of land estates. Their economic origins originated from frontier poverty to opulent wealth.

That being said: Then how do we explain the remarkable unanimity in their fundamental beliefs?

Although the level of those of formal training varied from spasmodic doses of home tutoring to the rigorous regiment of Harvard's classical studies; the debates in the Constitutional Convention and the writings of the founders project a far broader knowledge of religious, political, historical, economic and philosophical studies than would be found in any cross section of American leaders today. Perhaps the explanation will be found in the fact that they were all remarkably well read and mostly from the same books. Their historical readings included a broad perspective of Greek, Roman, Anglo-Saxon, European and English history. To me, nothing is more remarkable about the early American leaders than their breadth of reading and depth of knowledge concerning the essential elements of building.

These Founding Fathers were very careful students of the Bible, especially the Old Testament. Even though some did not belong to any Christian denomination, they held the teachings of Jesus in universal respect and admiration.

The United States was indeed begun by men who honored God and based their founding principles by the words of the Bible. For example, they lived their lives with honesty, reliability and fairness toward establishing this country "for the sake of its survival". A great many of the American founding fathers have been quoted regarding living by Biblical values. For example, Patrick Henry (1736-1799), a five times Governor of Virginia, whose "give me liberty or give me death" speech has made him immortal said: *"It cannot be emphasized too strongly, nor too often, that this great nation was founded not by religionists, but by Christians; not all religions, but on the gospel of Jesus Christ..."*.

Thomas Jefferson (1743-1826), was chosen to write the Declaration of Independence expressed his own opinion; *"I have little doubt that the whole country will soon be rallied to the unity of our Creator, and I hope, to the pure doctrines of Jesus also"*. He became the third President of the United States and in his 1805 inaugural address proclaimed that it was the God of the Bible. His exact words were: *"I shall need, too, the favor of that Being in whose hands we are, who are our forefathers, as Israel of old, from their native land and planted them in this country"*.

Is the American Constitution truly a godless Constitution?

The Founding Fathers, who wrote and ratified it, certainly didn't think so. Not only did several of the delegates openly acknowledge God's hand in its formation; many of them acknowledged specific biblical passages that directly affected its formation. For example, George Washington, Alexander Hamilton, and John Adams all credited *Jeremiah 18:9* for the principle undergirding the separation of powers. This principle and several other biblical passages including *Deuteronomy 17:15* were directly incorporated into the Constitution and the Article 2, Section 1 provision, that a President must be a natural born citizen. Then there was the Article 3, Section 3 Constitutional provision regarding witnesses and capital punishment in *Deuteronomy 17:6*, or Article 3, Section 3, Constitutional prohibition against attainder (i.e., against punishing the whole family for the acts of one of its members), and with *Ezekiel 18:20*. Several founders cited *Exodus 18:21* as the basis of Republicanism (type of government, not political party), found in Article 4, Section 4. *Ezra 7:24* established the type of tax exemptions that the founding fathers gave to our churches.[6] There are many other passages that provide direct influence on the Constitution, as you will see. This raises the question: *Why were the founding fathers so instrumental founding the Constitution and basing laws on religious principles?*

The first settlers to America came mostly from Europe primarily because the civil and religious leaders in Europe had wrongly taught the masses that the Bible authorized such atrocities being practiced there. It further authorized individual leaders of church and state to wield great and often tyrannical power over the people because they were illiterate. Therefore, they could not read scriptures to judge the authority and accuracy of what their leaders told them. They blindly believed and followed what they were being told and thus indirectly participated in the commission of those atrocities.

Learning from these tragedies, the American leaders were convinced that, if the common citizens could read and learn the word of God for themselves and study the limits on Government and authority set forth in the Bible, they would resist Government misbehavior and thus preclude similar occurrences in America.

It was from this history of abuse that so many religious settlers came to America which became a land to receive those persecuted from around the world. For example, in 1620, the Pilgrims came to America to escape the hounding persecution of England's King James. A decade later, after Puritan laymen in England received life sentences, had their noses slit, their ears cut off, and a brand placed on their foreheads, the 20,000 Puritans came to America. Similarly, in 1633, Catholics persecuted in England fled to America; in 1654, Jews persecuted and facing the Inquisition in Portugal fled to America; in 1680 Quakers fled to America after some 10,000 had been imprisoned or tortured in England for their faith; in 1683, persecuted German Anabaptist Mennonites (Moravians, Dunkers, etc.) fled to America; in 1685, Huguenots fled France (some 400,000) to avoid death and persecution from religious leaders there; and in 1731, 20,000 Lutherans fled to America after being expelled from Austria. This story of persecution has often been repeated across the pages of history. America indeed was and still is a place of asylum for the benefit of those and the rest of the world who were persecuted for their faith in God.

With this background, and having set forth the purpose of the law and the evil it was designed to prevent, the early colonies needed a law requiring public schools to be started in each community to provide students a good academic education based on God's word. This Bible-centered emphasis was common in education and in subsequent education laws as well. This was a fact confirmed by the records from visitors to America. For example, the Connecticut legislature had been concerned about the illiteracy because, if a child could not read, he would not know the word of God or the laws of the state. Therefore, if the legislature enacted a law that contradicted the word of God, and if citizens were illiterate and uneducated about the proper role of civil government as set forth in the Scriptures, they would not prevent the passage of an inappropriate law.

The Founders believed that schools and education systems were proper means to encourage the religion, morality and knowledge necessary for good government and the happiness of mankind. Our early education system was remarkable. There is an old saying that says: **"The philosophy of the school room in one generation will be the philosophy of government in the next".** It is appropriate to examine closely the educational philosophy and analyze the influence of laws which were created to protect its citizens, that produced the longest ongoing constitutional republic in the history of the world.

Remember the United States is a limited Republic, not a Democracy. *What's the difference you ask?* A democracy becomes increasingly unwieldy and inefficient as the population grows. A republic, on the other hand, governs through elected representatives and can be expanded indefinitely. James Madison, fourth President of the United States, in the Federalist papers, number 14 page 100, said, *"In a democracy the people meet and exercise the government in person; in a republic they assemble and administer it by their representatives and agents. A democracy, consequently, must be confined to a small spot. A republic may be extended over a large region."*

To make his position completely clear, Madison offered a precise definition of a republic as follows: *"We may define a republic to be…a government which derives all its powers directly or indirectly from the great body of the people, and is administered by persons holding their offices during pleasure for a limited period, or during good behavior. It is essential to such a government that it be derived from the great body of the society, not from an inconsiderable portion or a favored class of it; otherwise a handful of tyrannical nobles, exercising their oppressions by a delegation of their powers, might aspire to the rank of republicans and claim for their government the honorable title of republic."*[7]

During the period since the founding of the country, an ideological war erupted, and the word "democracy" became one of the casualties. Today, the average American uses the term "democracy" to describe America's traditional Constitutional republic. But technically speaking, it is not. The Founders had hoped that their descendants would maintain a clear distinction between a democracy and a republic.

What was the educational philosophy of the schools from which our early leaders graduated?

We all know that the first pilgrims to arrive in the country, came from Europe, England in particular, where they wanted a freedom to worship as they chose rather than as ordered by the ruling class. They brought with them their own Bibles and values that they wanted their children to read and follow.

The settlers followed the old adage that says, *"The philosophy of the schoolroom in one generation will be the philosophy of government in the next."* So, what was the educational philosophy of the early schools? What schools did the founders of the American Republic attend?

It was one of the first schools that was opened to educate the people of the New World. Harvard was founded in 1636; but, do you know why it was founded???

Harvard was established as a school to train ministers of the Bible! Its two mottoes, *"For Christ and the Church"* and *"For the Glory of Christ"* signified that it was established to help students put Christ as "…the foundation of…knowledge and learning." Consistent with those two mottos, the Harvard administration gave its students these instructions, *"let every student be plainly instructed and …consider well, the main end of his life and studies is to know God and Jesus, which is the eternal life, (John 17:3), and therefore to lay Christ in the bottom as the only foundation of all sound knowledge and learning".*[8] The early Harvard administration instituted specific educational practices including: *"Everyone shall so exercise himself in reading the Scriptures twice a day that he shall be ready to give such an account of his proficiency therein".[9]*

Since, Harvard was a school that trained many of those who established our government, its philosophy based on the foundation of Biblical principles had enormous impact. Leaders such as John Hancock, John Adams, Samuel Adams, William Ellery, William Hooper, Robert Paine and Elbridge Gerry were graduates of Harvard. I'll bet you don't recognize many of these names. Do you? They were among the signers of the Declaration of Independence in 1776!

See if you recognize these other names who were Harvard graduates: William Samuel Johnson, Rufus King, Fisher Ames (Framer of the Bill of Rights), William Cushing (an original US Supreme Court Justice), or Timothy Pickering (the Secretary of War for Presidents George Washington and John Adams)? What are they best known for? They signed the original Constitution of the United States.

Harvard essentially established our philosophy of government. Obviously, its academic endeavors were built upon the foundation of Biblical principles.

Yale, established in 1701, was another school founded on Christian principles began as a school to train ministers of the Bible. Like Harvard, Yale instructed its students: *"Above all, have an eye to the great end of all of your studies which is to obtain the clearest conceptions of divine things and to lead you to a saving knowledge of God and His son Jesus Christ".*[10] Again like Harvard, Yale stated: *"All scholars are required to live a religious and blameless life according to the rules of God's word, diligently reading the Holy Scriptures…and constantly attending all the duties of religion".*[11] So both Yale and Harvard provided an education based on Christian principles and knowing Christ.

Do the names: Lyman Hall, Philip Livingston, Lewis Morris, or Oliver Wolcott mean anything to you? I didn't think so. These men, who were graduates of Yale, signed the Declaration of Independence.

Not to be outdone by Harvard, Yale graduated these great men in its early classes: Abraham Baldwin, Jared Ingersoll, William Livingston, Noah Webster (remember him and his dictionaries?), Zephaniah Swift (author of the first Legal Text in America) and James Kent (called the Father of American Jurisprudence). Who were they? They also signed the Constitution of the United States

The Presbyterian Synod established a school in New Jersey in 1746, which produced many outstanding early leaders of the country. Perhaps this school, now named Princeton University, produced more early national leaders than any other. It also was started as a school to train ministers of the Gospel. It produced many signers of the Declaration of Independence, the Constitution and members of the Supreme Court.

What was required of the students at Princeton?

"Every student shall attend worship in the college hall morning and evening…(and) shall attend public worship on the Sabbath… There shall be assigned to each class certain exercises for their religious instruction… No student belonging to any class shall neglect them".[12]

Can you imagine a school today with this requirement???

Interestingly, a scholar from Scotland named Rev. John Witherspoon became president of the University in 1768 and personally trained many of these future leaders. Do you know what else Rev. Witherspoon was famous for? He too signed the Declaration of Independence! John Witherspoon probably trained more American leaders than any other individual including a U.S. President, a U.S Vice President, three Supreme Court Justices, 13 governors, and 50 congressmen---not to mention many residential cabinet members. Rev. Witherspoon has rightly been called the "Educational Father of many Founding Fathers."[13]

As a leading educator of all time, Dr. Witherspoon taught that government was merely a reflection of its citizens; and, if, Americans became profane or immoral, their government would also become profane and immoral. History has confirmed Dr. Witherpoon's teaching that such governments do not survive. Remember the Roman era, the Ottoman era, the era of Stalin and Hitler? *None survived!*

It was former Princeton graduate Elias Boudinot (a framer of the Bill of Rights in the first Congress) who stated: *"If the moral character of a people once degenerates, their political character must soon follow."*[14]

These were the first educational institutions in America. So what was the foundation recognized by all of the early leaders as the true foundation of successful American government??? It simply was the principles of religion and morality and not constitutions and laws! All of the forefathers knew and understood this. Signer of the Declaration of Independence, Charles Carroll said, *"Without morals, a republic cannot subsist any length of time; they therefore who are decrying the Christian religion, whose morality is so sublime and pure...are undermining the solid foundation of morals, the best security for the duration of a free government."*[15]

Unknown by many was that Dr. Witherspoon, and other academic and government leaders of the time, personally trained black students and women in these principles. Francis Hopkinson and Benjamin Franklin *(remember him?)*, both of whom were signers of the Declaration of Independence, were involved in the development of education for black students both in academics and in the principles of Christianity.[16] Another signer of the Declaration of Independence, Benjamin Rush, not only promoted black education,[17] he also promoted open education for women and was closely involved in the first American school to educate women.[18]

It is interesting to note that virtually every one of the 55 founding fathers who framed the Constitution were members of orthodox Christian churches.[19] Many of these founding fathers were outspoken evangelicals.

Similarly, of the 56 founding fathers who signed the Declaration of Independence in 1776, over half had received degrees from schools that today would be considered seminaries or Bible schools.[20] It was the signers of the Declaration of Independence who started the Sunday school movement as well as several Bible societies and missionary societies in America. They were also responsible for penning numerous religious works and publishing many famous Bibles.

Before the Revolution when Americans were still British citizens, it had been illegal to print English language Bibles in America. That policy terminated with the final American victory over the British at Yorktown. A Philadelphia printer then approached Congress seeking permission to print an English language Bible on his premises. He pointed out that it would be *"a neat edition of the Holy Scriptures for the use of schools".*[21] It is interesting that the first Bible printed in America, in English, was printed by Congress for the use by our schools. In the front cover of the Bible, it says *"Resolve that the United States and Congress assembled recommend this edition of the Bible to the inhabitants of the United States".* **Note, the first**

Bible printed in English in America was approved by the gentlemen who signed the Declaration of Independence and the Constitution, endorsed by Congress and done for the use of schools. *Isn't it interesting, that today we are told that the government does not want any kind of religion in education!*

The framers of our Constitution did not believe that encouraging religion in schools was unconstitutional; rather, they believed just the opposite. Only in recent decades have courts ruled otherwise. Today we are told that America had no godly heritage and that our founding fathers were atheist, agnostic and deists who formed a completely secular government. However, a clear pronouncement by our founding father, John Adams, provides otherwise. Adams declared: *"The general principle on which the fathers achieved independence were…the general principles of Christianity".*[22]

According to John Quincy Adams on the 4th of July 1776, the founders had taken the principles that came into the world through the birth of Christ and used them to birth the nation thus joining together Christian principles and civil government in an *"indissoluble bond"*. It is interesting to note that today's ivory tower elite **assert just the opposite**… they wrongly claim that the founders did not want an indissoluble bond, but rather, they wanted a so-called *"separation"* in order to keep Biblical principles out of civil government. However, the Founding Fathers' own records document their steadfast conviction that Christian principles were to be preserved in the civil arena.

John Jay provides a clear example. He was president of the Continental Congress during the Revolution and was one of the three Founding Fathers who drafted and signed the Peace Treaty with Great Britain to establish America as an independent nation. After the Constitution was written, Jay helped pen the Federalist Papers and is considered one of the three men most responsible for the adoption of the Constitution. When George Washington became President, Jay was appointed the original Chief Justice of the United States Supreme Court.

Chief Justice John Jay, believing that Christian principles should be included in civil arenas declared: *"Providence has given to our people the choice of their rules; and it is the duty…as well as the privilege and interest…*

of our Christian nation to select and prefer Christians for their rulers".[23]

The Biblical foundation of America is so obvious to previous generations that in 1892 the United States Supreme Court had no difficulty in rendering a unanimous decision declaring: *"No purpose of action against religion can be imputed to any legislation, state or national, because this is a religious people…this is a Christian nation".*[24]

Can you imagine what in the world would lead the United States Supreme Court to conclude that America was a Christian nation?

The simple answer is American's own history. The court decision in the **Church of the Holy Trinity v United States** (1892)[25] case was only 16 pages long; but, even in that short span, the court provided almost **80 different historical precedents**. The court cited statements of the Founding Fathers, acts of Congress, state governments and numerous other official documents. The Court noted that there were many additional volumes of historical precedents supporting that America was a Christian nation. Eighty precedents in a case is not only impressive, but also important for courts seeking to base their decisions on precedent. The courts use precedents from earlier decisions to enable them to be consistent from ruling to ruling; thus, contributing to a stable society. *(Remember this very important statement for future reference in this book!!!)*

So what I am saying is that our Founding Fathers pioneered an education system based on Judeo/Christian principles and ideals for all people regardless of race or gender! The principles taught in the Bible and the Torah, strongly believed in by the Founding Fathers as divinely inspired, and followed in their governing documents, are the foundations of this republic. That is what has made this country so great. What happened to all these once great institutions and their belief systems to cause them to remove these principles and foundation upon which they were founded? Read on and you will see!

Significantly, that 1892 court decision was by no means the only Supreme Court decision that recognized and preserved America's Biblical heritage. Similar decisions were rendered both before and after that ruling. This Biblical basis for the laws of America has been seriously diminished over the years as will be documented in the following chapters. As you continue reading, just remember that the foundation of the laws of the United States were made based upon Judeo-Christian principles.

Chapter 2

Early Laws Of Education

The philosophy of the early leaders was based in religion and moral ideals from educational laws that began a century-and-a-half earlier in what was to become America. Remember, that the original pilgrims to this country left Europe because of the atrocities they had experienced before leaving and that they were willing to sacrifice their lives to escape those persecutions for their faiths.

The leaders of the time wrongly taught the people that the Bible authorized these atrocities. It was up to the governing authorities and certain church leaders to control the situation with their great power. It wasn't just one religion or faith that was being persecuted. For example: the Pilgrims came to America in 1620 to escape the persecution of England's King James, and 10 years later, the Puritans also came to America after Puritan laymen in England received life sentences *(as well as having their noses slit, ears cut off, and foreheads branded)*. In 1632, Catholics persecuted in England fled to America. In 1654, Jews persecuted by Catholics and facing the Inquisition in Portugal fled to America. In 1680, after many thousands had been imprisoned and tortured in England for their faith, Quakers fled to America. Further, in 1685, persecuted German Anabaptists (Mennonites, Moravians, Dunkers, etc.) fled to America as did the Lutherans after being expelled from Austria. This story of persecutions has been repeated since the earliest days of the Bible. Everyone believed America was a place of rest and escape from the rest of the world gone mad with its persecution for faith in God.

These early pioneers knew that widespread lack of Biblical knowledge and illiteracy of the majority of people controlled by ruthless governments and leaders back in Europe were at the root of these persecutions. They learned from their experiences in Europe and decided to teach common people to read and learn the Word of God.

Knowing and applying Biblical principles and guidelines does not prevent all atrocities; however, it probably reduces them. Some critics argue that there were atrocities brought in the name of Christianity such as the Salem Witch trials, the torture of the Moors, the Inquisition, and yes, even the World War II Holocaust (which some Jews attribute to Christians because Hitler, in his youth, was a member of a Christian church...however, it was recently proven that Hitler was very anti-Christian and that his Nazis engaged regularly in an effort to remove Christianity.[26] It is interesting to note that, Hitler killed more than twice as many Christians as Jews![27]

The plan of the pioneers was to prevent atrocities by teaching a knowledge of the Scriptures based in experience and knowledge. With this plan setting forth the prevention of evil, the pioneers required that the public schools in each community teach a sound academic program based on God's Word. Both historically and statistically, it is provable that while Christianity does not make a man perfect, it tends to restrain their inherent destructive behavior. Ben Franklin once reminded religious critic Thomas Paine that *"If men are so wicked with religion, what would they be if without it?"*[28]

A Frenchman visitor to America, Alexis de Tocqueville, when studying what was making this country great, wrote that the religious aspect of American public education was the major cause of its (America's) remarkable rise and progress as a nation.[29] His writing today is known as *Democracy in America*.

Isn't it interesting that the Founders of our country encouraged the study of religion, required schools to teach religion, and passed the First Amendment to the Constitution, which is the very Amendment to the Constitution that courts now interpret as prohibiting the presence of religious activity in public education? (The First Amendment to the United States Constitution is part of the Bill of Rights. The amendment states: **"Congress shall make no law respecting an establishment of religion, or** *prohibiting the free exercise thereof; or abridging the freedom of speech, or of the press; or the right of the people peaceably to assemble, and to petition the Government for a redress of grievances.")*

Did you know that the Organic Laws of the United States of America lists America's four fundamental laws as: (1) The Articles of Confederation; (2) The Declaration of Independence; (3) The Constitution of the United States; and (4) the Northwest Ordinance. *(US Code Annotated).*

Bet you never heard of the Northwest Ordinance. *Right?*

It was the first federal law to address education and was passed at the same time and by the same Founding Fathers who wrote the First Amendment to the Constitution. The Northwest Ordinance (formally *An Ordinance for the Government of the Territory of the United States, North-West of the River Ohio*, and also known as the *Freedom Ordinance* or "The Ordinance of 1787") was an act of the Congress of the Confederation of the United States was passed July 13, 1787. The primary effect of the ordinance was the creation of the Northwest Territory as the first organized territory of the United States out of the region south of the Great Lakes, north and west of the Ohio River, and east of the Mississippi River.

Many of the concepts and guarantees of the Ordinance of 1787 were incorporated in the U.S. Constitution and the Bill of Rights. In the Northwest Territory, various legal and property rights were enshrined, religious tolerance was proclaimed, and it was stated that since *"Religion, morality, and knowledge, being necessary to good government and the happiness of mankind, schools and the means of education shall forever be encouraged."* The first education law recognized that schools and education systems were a proper means to encourage *"…the religion, morality, and knowledge"* that was *"…so necessary to good government and the happiness of mankind…."* The founders of our government did not believe that encouraging religion was unconstitutional; rather, they believed just the opposite. Unfortunately the courts have ruled otherwise.

The founders of our country and our various states recognized this law in all of the initial state constitutions and that compliance was a prerequisite for the admission of a territory or state into the Union.

Alabama 1901, Preamble: "We the people of the State of Alabama, invoking the favor and guidance of Almighty God, do ordain and establish the following Constitution."

Alaska 1956, Preamble: "We, the people of Alaska , grateful to God and to those who founded our nation and pioneered this great land."

Arizona 1911, Preamble: "We, the people of the State of Arizona, grateful to Almighty God for our liberties, do ordain this Constitution..."

Arkansas 1874, Preamble: "We, the people of the State of Arkansas, grateful to Almighty God for the privilege of choosing our own form of government..."

California 1879, Preamble: "We, the People of the State of California, grateful to Almighty God for our freedom..."

Colorado 1876, Preamble: "We, the people of Colorado, with profound reverence for the Supreme Ruler of the Universe..."

Connecticut 1818, Preamble: "The People of Connecticut, acknowledging with gratitude the good Providence of God in permitting them to enjoy."

Delaware 1897, Preamble: "Through Divine Goodness all men have, by nature, the rights of worshiping and serving their Creator according to the dictates of their consciences."

Florida 1885, Preamble: "We, the people of the State of Florida, grateful to Almighty God for our constitutional liberty, establish this Constitution..."

Georgia 1777, Preamble: "We, the people of Georgia, relying upon protection and guidance of Almighty God, do ordain and establish this Constitution..."

Hawaii 1959, Preamble: "We, the people of Hawaii, Grateful for Divine Guidance ... Establish this Constitution."

Idaho 1889, Preamble: "We, the people of the State of Idaho, grateful to Almighty God for our freedom, to secure its blessings"

Illinois 1870, Preamble: "We, the people of the State of Illinois, grateful to Almighty God for the civil , political and religious liberty which He hath so long permitted us to enjoy and looking to Him for a blessing on our endeavors."

Indiana 1851, Preamble: "We, the People of the State of Indiana, grateful to Almighty God for the free exercise of the right to choose our form of government."

Iowa 1857, Preamble: "We, the People of the State of Iowa, grateful to the Supreme Being for the blessings hitherto enjoyed, and feeling our dependence on Him for a continuation of these blessings, establish this Constitution."

Kansas 1859, Preamble: "We, the people of Kansas, grateful to Almighty God for our civil and religious privileges establish this Constitution."

Kentucky 1891, Preamble: "We, the people of the Commonwealth are grateful to Almighty God for the civil, political and religious liberties..."

Louisiana 1921, Preamble: "We, the people of the State of Louisiana, grateful to Almighty God for the civil, political and religious liberties we enjoy."

Maine 1820, Preamble: "We the People of Maine acknowledging with grateful hearts the goodness of the Sovereign Ruler of the Universe in affording us an opportunity. And imploring His aid and direction."

Maryland 1776, Preamble: "We, the people of the State of Maryland, grateful to Almighty God for our civil and religious liberty..."

Massachusetts 1780, Preamble: "We...the people of Massachusetts, acknowledging with grateful hearts, the goodness of the Great Legislator of the Universe in the course of His Providence, an opportunity and devoutly imploring His direction ."

Michigan 1908, Preamble: "We, the people of the State of Michigan, grateful to Almighty God for the blessings of freedom establish this Constitution."

Minnesota, 1857, Preamble: "We, the people of the State of Minnesota, grateful to God for our civil and religious liberty, and desiring to perpetuate its blessings."

Mississippi 1890, Preamble: "We, the people of Mississippi in convention assembled, grateful to Almighty God, and invoking His blessing on our work."

Missouri 1845, Preamble: "We, the people of Missouri, with profound reverence for the Supreme Ruler of the Universe, and grateful for His goodness establish this Constitution..."

Montana 1889, Preamble: "We, the people of Montana, grateful to Almighty God for the blessings of liberty establish this Constitution."

Nebraska 1875, Preamble: "We, the people, grateful to Almighty God for our freedom . Establish this Constitution."

Nevada 1864, Preamble: "We the people of the State of Nevada, grateful to Almighty God for our freedom, establish this Constitution..." "

New Hampshire 1792, Part I. Art. I. Sec.V: "Every individual has a natural and unalienable right to worship God according to the dictates of his own conscience."

New Jersey 1844, Preamble: " We, the people of the State of New Jersey, grateful to Almighty God for civil and religious liberty which He hath so long permitted us to enjoy, and looking to Him for a blessing on our endeavors."

New Mexico 1911, Preamble: "We, the People of New Mexico, grateful to Almighty God for the blessings of liberty…"

New York 1846, Preamble: "We, the people of the State of New York, grateful to Almighty God for our freedom, in order to secure its blessings."

North Carolina 1868, Preamble: "We, the people of the State of North Carolina, grateful to Almighty God, the Sovereign Ruler of Nations, for our civil, political, and religious liberties, and acknowledging our dependence upon Him for the continuance of those..."

North Dakota 1889, Preamble: "We, the people of North Dakota, grateful to Almighty God for the blessings of civil and religious liberty, do ordain..."

Ohio 1852, Preamble: "We the people of the state of Ohio, grateful to Almighty God for our freedom, to secure its blessings and to promote our common..."

Oklahoma 1907, Preamble: "Invoking the guidance of Almighty God, in order to secure and perpetuate the blessings of liberty, establish this …"

Oregon 1857, Bill of Rights, Article I , Section 2: "All men shall be secure in the Natural right, to worship Almighty God according to the dictates of their consciences."

Pennsylvania 1776, Preamble: "We, the people of Pennsylvania, grateful to Almighty God for the blessings of civil and religious liberty, and humbly invoking His guidance... "

Rhode Island 1842, Preamble: "We the People of the State of Rhode Island grateful to Almighty God for the civil and religious liberty which He hath so long permitted us to enjoy, and looking to Him for a blessing... "

South Carolina 1778, Preamble: "We, the people of the State of South Carolina grateful to God for our liberties, do ordain and establish this Constitution."

South Dakota 1889, Preamble: "We, the people of South Dakota, grateful to Almighty God for our civil and religious liberties…"

Tennessee 1796, Art. XI.III: "That all men have a natural and indefeasible right to worship Almighty God according to the dictates of their conscience... "

Texas 1845, Preamble: "We the People of the Republic of Texas, acknowledging, with gratitude, the grace and beneficence of God…"

Utah 1896, Preamble: "Grateful to Almighty God for life and liberty, we establish this Constitution.

Vermont 1777, Preamble: "Whereas all government ought to enable the individuals who compose it to enjoy their natural rights, and other blessings which the Author of Existence has bestowed on man…"

Virginia 1776, Bill of Rights: "XVI Religion, or the Duty which we owe our Creator can be directed only by Reason and that it is the mutual duty of all to practice Christian Forbearance, Love and Charity towards each other. "

Washington 1889, Preamble: "We the People of the State of Washington, grateful to the Supreme Ruler of the Universe for our liberties, do ordain this Constitution."

West Virginia 1872, Preamble: "Since through Divine Providence we enjoy the blessings of civil, political and religious liberty, we, the people of West Virginia reaffirm our faith in and constant reliance upon God …"

Wisconsin 1848, Preamble: "We, the people of Wisconsin, grateful to Almighty God for our freedom, domestic tranquility…"

Wyoming 1890, Preamble: "We, the people of the State of Wyoming, grateful to God for our civil, political, and religious liberties, establish this Constitution…"

After reviewing acknowledgments of God from all 50 state constitutions, one is faced with the prospect that maybe, the **ACLU and the out-of-control federal courts are wrong!**

(Note, that at no time is anyone ever told that they MUST worship God.)

"Those people who will not be governed by God will be ruled by tyrants," stated William Penn.

It is very obvious, and historically viewed, that American education was *"...nurtured in the lap of the church."*[30] Then, as the country grew and the population increased, *"the church reluctantly relinquished her claim upon the elementary schools."*[31] Even though the jurisdictional authority over education had been partially shifted to the States, the philosophy of education remain unchanged.

Do you remember Daniel Webster? He served 30 years in Congress, was Secretary of State for three different Presidents, and personally argued and won numerous decisions before the US Supreme Court. One of these Supreme Court cases, **Vidal v Girard (1844)**[32], dealt with a Pennsylvania case in which all ministers were forbidden to teach in a public school in the Philadelphia area. It was believed that this was an attempt by the school to prevent religious instruction at the school. In his argument before the Court, Webster told the Court: *"When little children were brought in to the presence of the Son of God, His disciples proposed to send them away, but Jesus said, 'Suffer the little children to come unto Me.' (Matt.19:14) Unto Me!!!...and that injunction is of permanent obligation; it addresses itself today with the same earnestness and the same authority which attended its first utterance to the Christian world. It is of force everywhere and at all times; it extends to the ends of the earth, it will reach to the end of time always and everywhere sounding in the ears of men with an...authority which nothing can supersede. 'Suffer little children to come unto Me!'"*[33]

Daniel Webster opposed any education that excluded religious instruction! The US Supreme Court ruled in a unanimous decision written by Justice Joseph Story which said in part:

"Why may not the Bible and especially the New Testament, without note or comment, be read and taught as Divine revelation in the school, its general precepts expounded...and its glorious principles of morality incul-

cated?...*Where can the purest principles of morality be learned or so clearly or so perfectly as from the New Testament?*"[34]

So in the middle 1800's the US Supreme Court was protecting the teaching of the Bible in public schools that had been introduced into America more than 200 years earlier.

Did you know that well into the 20th century that it was the practice of State universities and colleges to conduct chapel services; chapel attendance was required, at about half of the schools, and at a quarter of these schools even required both regular church attendance and add chapel services?

Why?

Dr. Benjamin Rush, who was a signer of the Declaration of Independence, founded 5 colleges and served in three presidential administrations, was the first to propose nationwide public schools. He was called *"The Father of Public Schools under the Constitution,"* and saw the Bible as the only sure means to prevent crime, for it dealt with the heart—the source of all crime. Therefore, Dr. Rush accurately warned that if America ceased to teach the Bible in schools, then not only would crime increase but great quantities of time and money would be spent in fighting it. *History has proven Dr. Rush right!!!*

Fisher Ames, who was mentioned earlier, helped frame the Bill of Rights and the First Amendment to the Constitution, was an early leader in education of America. He once wrote an article on education where he noted a dangerous unintended consequence of adding more books to a schools' curriculum. He explained that each time a new book was added to the classroom time was spent on that new book. The growing amount of time spent on the many new books could eventually reduce the amount of time spent on the Bible. *"Why then,"* he wrote, *"if these books for children must be retained, should not the Bible regain the place it once held in a school book? Its morals are pure; its examples, captivating and noble. The reverence for the Sacred Book that is thus early impressed lasts long, and probably if not impressing in infancy, never takes firm hold of the mind."*[35]

For several hundred years, American education included religious and moral principles as a part of its educational structure and curriculum. There is no question of the academic success of that theory or philosophy.

In the 1950's, more than 100 years after Webster's winning decision in the Supreme Court, the Court continued to keep a similar position toward religious teaching in public schools, stating:

"*When the State encourages religious instruction, or cooperates with religious authorities by adjusting the schedule of public events to sectarian needs, it follows the best of our traditions. For it then respects the religious nature of our people and accommodates the public service for their spiritual needs. To hold that it may not would be to find in the Constitution a requirement that the government show a callous indifference to religious groups. That would be preferring those who believe in no religion over those who do believe... We find no such constitutional requirement.*"[36]

For nearly 400 years, the American education system included religious and moral principles as a part of its teachings; but, as you will soon see, the courts began to order a completely non-Christian/non-religion approach to public education.

After the expulsion of any religious and moral teaching in schools since about 1962, the educational scores of students have plummeted and the violent acts of students in schools have risen dramatically.[37] Another indicator of the present condition of education in America is that illiteracy has gone through the roof!!! America now ranks 27th in the world in literacy among 200 nations.[38] Just a few decades ago America had one of the highest literacy rates. Now, according to testimony before Congress, illiteracy is now so rampant that among recent high school graduates many were unable to read their own diplomas!!!

Have you tried reading any of your children or grand children's text messages recently? Could you understand them? How many people under the age of 40 even read a newspaper today?

David Barton, nationally known historian and educator, wrote in his book, "*Four Centuries of American Education*", the following: "*For four centuries in American education, the three essential elements of religion, morality and knowledge formed the basis of character and achievement; experience and common sense demonstrate that these elements still provide the foundation that will enable today's student to be the solid citizens not only to protect the proven educational philosophy that made and has kept America great but also to do everything that we can to transmit that successful educa-*

tional philosophy to future generations, just as our forebears did throughout the first four centuries of American education."[39]

Chapter 3

Changing Times

Beginning with the Pilgrims in the 1600's, the American system of government was built upon religion and morality and has enjoyed unprecedented success. The system of American government as a **constitutional republic** (notice I didn't say *democracy*) has existed more than 235 years using the same governing document. It is interesting to note that during this same period while we have had just one government; Russia has had five, Poland seven, France fifteen, etc.

While every nation has had access to the same body of governing principles, information and philosophies when forming their governments, none chose those of our Founding Fathers whose principles and philosophies were so successfully implemented in our Constitution. It is not surprising that the US Constitution is based on many Biblical principles. There are numerous Biblical teachings and principles upon which the Constitution was based. For example, Isaiah 33:22 sets forth three distinct branches of government! The separation of powers between the three branches was based on teaching from Jeremiah 18:9. The basis for tax exemption for churches is found in Ezra 7:24.

In 1892, in the case of ***The Holy Trinity vs The United States***,[40] the US Supreme Court in another unanimous decision declared: *No purpose of action against religion can be imputed to any legislation, state or national because this is a religious people…This is a Christian nation."*

One of the interesting things about this decision is that the Court cited 80, **that's 80**, different historical precedents to reach its conclusion that America was a Christian nation. This was not only impressive, but very important because most courts base their decisions on precedence so their rulings are consistent which contribute to a stable society.

There was an interesting state case in 1811 in New York which the US Supreme Court ultimately upheld. The case involved a man who had distributed a pamphlet full of vulgar and malicious profanity attacking God, Jesus Christ, and the Bible. He was fined and punished by the court. On appeal, the New York State Supreme Court upheld the conviction and stated that:

"Whatever strikes at the root of Christianity tends manifestly to the dissolution of civil government!"[41]

Today, all we hear is "separation of church and state". The First Amendment states:

"Congress shall make no law respecting an establishment of r eligion or prohibiting the free exercise thereof."

Notice there are **no words** of *"separation," "Church,"* or *"state"* found in any part of the First Amendment to the Constitution. In fact, that phrase, *"separation of church and state"* **does not appear in ANY governmental founding document!** The purpose of the wording in the First Amendment was to limit the federal government, NOT the people from establishing any national religion. Secondly, the government could not stop public religious expressions but must protect them.

When the Founding Fathers wrote the Constitution of the United States (our governing document), they created three distinct branches of government: The Executive (President and his staff); the Legislative (both Houses of Congress); and the Judicial (the Supreme Court and the courts and legal system). The original intent was that the Legislative branch would enact laws and treaties that would then be sent to the Executive branch to sign into law or to be vetoed (which can be overridden by the Congress). The Executive branch via the President is responsible for implementing and enforcing the laws written by the Legislative branch via Congress, and, to that end, appoints the heads of the federal agencies, including the Cabinet. The Judicial branch would interpret the laws based on the Constitution. That was their intent.

Today, under Article II of the Constitution, the President is responsible for the execution and enforcement of the laws created by Congress. Fifteen executive departments — each led by an appointed member of the President's Cabinet — carry out the day-to-day administration of the federal government. They are joined in this by other executive agencies such as the CIA and Environmental Protection Agency, the heads of which are not part of the Cabinet, but who are under the full authority of the President. The President also appoints the heads of more than 50 independent federal commissions, such as the Federal Reserve Board or the Securities and Exchange Commission, as well as federal judges, ambassadors, and other federal offices. The Executive Office of the President (EOP) consists of the immediate staff to the President, along with entities such as the Office of Management and Budget and the Office of the United States Trade Representative.

Established by Article I of the Constitution, the Legislative Branch consists of the House of Representatives and the Senate, which together, form the United States Congress. The Legislative Branch has 535 members of Congress consisting of 100 Senators and 435 members of the House of Representatives. The Constitution grants Congress the **sole** authority to enact legislation and declare war, the right to confirm or reject many Presidential appointments, and has substantial investigative powers. While the Executive and Legislative branches are **elected** by the people, members of the Judicial Branch are **appointed** by the President and confirmed by the Senate. **Therein lies part of the problem the American public faces.** A President can appoint members of the judiciary that follow his governing philosophy whether liberal or conservative; and, if Congress approves them, these judges and justices, appointed for life, will determine the interpretation of the laws under the Constitution.

Article III of the Constitution, which establishes the Judicial Branch leaves Congress significant discretion to determine the shape and structure of the federal judiciary. Even the number of Supreme Court Justices is left to Congress — at times there have been as few as six, while the current number (nine, with one Chief Justice and eight Associate Justices) has only been in place since 1869. The Constitution also grants Congress the power to establish courts inferior to the Supreme Court. To that end, Congress has established the United States District courts, which try most federal cases, and the 13 United States Courts of Appeals which review appealed district court cases before they are eligible for review by the US Supreme Court.

Federal judges can only be removed through impeachment by the House of Representatives and conviction in the Senate. These judges and justices serve no fixed term — they serve lifetime appointments, or until retirement, or conviction by the Senate. By design, this insulates them from the temporary passions of the public and allows them to apply the law with only justice in mind and not electoral or political concerns.

The nine member Supreme Court can rule on an act or new law enacted by Congress and signed by the President to be unconstitutional and thus the law is voided. **So get the picture, a majority of Congress' 535 members passes a new law, the President signs the law BUT, five of the nine member Supreme Court can nullify the law!**

Now who is actually controlling the country??

Think about the question placed before you in the Introduction: **"If you wanted to take over a country without firing a single shot and time was not critical, how would you do it?"** A partial answer is to remove religion from the daily lives of a country's people. Religion gives people hope and a moral compass to follow teaching them right from wrong. Without a religious belief system foundation, there is no moral compass and the public is basically without regard to right and wrong…good and evil. As a result the culture begins to crumble.

Is that what is happening to America? Is this why we have lost our moral compass? Read the next several chapters and make your own determination.

Chapter 4

Attacks On Education

Today, America has no moral compass. *(I keep repeating that so you won't forget it!)* For nearly 150 years, the Courts and Congress have relied on the moral law as the basis for our civil laws. Although many today state that you cannot legislate morality, such charges are utter nonsense. Every law that exists is the legislation of morality. As a signer of the Declaration of Independence, John Witherspoon explained: *"Consider all morality in general as conforming to a law".* Consequently, it is never a matter **if** morality can be legislated, only **whose** morality can be legislated. The Founders of the Constitution believed the Bible to be the perfect example of moral legislation and the source of what they called the moral law.[42]

So when and where did the morality of America begin to change because of attacks on religion?

For many years there has been an attempt to secularize *(remove all religion)* the education and morality of the United States. The first major event to drastically change the separation of church and state was the 1947 Supreme Court case of **Everson v. Board of Education of Ewing Township**.[43] In this case, Ewing Township enacted a policy where they reimbursed parents for the cost of public bus transportation of children to and from school. This policy was enacted pursuant to a state law permitting local school districts to provide transportation of children and gave these school districts authority to devise rules and enter into contracts for such transportation. When a local resident, Everson, learned that part of the school's policy was to also reimburse transportation costs to parents whose children attended Catholic Parochial schools, he brought suit through his capacity as a district tax payer upon. Children attending Parochial schools were taught the tenants and modes of worship of Catholicism along with secular education. The Plaintiff alleged that, by sending the children to church schools, public interest in the general education did not follow the due process clause because tax payers were paying to satisfy the personal desires of the parents; therefore, the statute and resolution violated the state and Federal Constitution.

One of the issues to be decided by the Court was: *Does a law violate the First Amendment "Establishment clause" when citizens are forced to pay taxes to supplement the support and maintenance of schools that are dedicated to and teaches the Catholic faith?*

The court held NO. It ruled that parents are entitled to choose where their children attend school, be it religious or non-religious, so long as the school at issue meets the state educational requirements. The state does not support the school nor does it contribute money to the religious schools for support. Through legislation, the state merely provides a means of transportation to and from school for needy parents to ensure that their children get to school safely. Thus, under its legislation, all children are entitled to safe and efficient transportation regardless of religion which is, not a matter of religion, but a matter of public welfare. However, in reaching its decision in this case, the Court made it clear that there must be a separation of church and state, and that any such cross of the two would not be tolerated.

Justice Black, writing for the Court, explained that the Establishment Clause was enacted when religious persecution was at the forefront of issues facing the early settlers of America who were searching for a haven where they would be able to "escape the bondage of laws which compel them to support and attend government favored churches." The charters granted by the English Crown gave certain individuals and companies the authority to govern the Colonies and to establish a religion that every person would be compelled to follow. The Colonies were required to pay tithes and taxes to maintain the established church and taught to hate those who did not go along. These Colonies became increasingly enraged at the injustice of being required to serve the specific church. James Madison and Thomas Jefferson both strongly opposed this and led a fight against the tax for the church. The Court quotes Madison in his memorable writing against the law saying… *"In it he eloquently argued that a true religion did not need the support of law; that no person, either believer or nonbeliever, should be taxed to support a religious institution of any kind; that the minds of men always be wholly be free; and that cruel persecutions were an inevitable result of government established religion."*

Further, the First Amendment provides for the safety of Americans in that it prohibits the establishment of a religion by the government. It prohibits the government from suppressing any individual free exercise of religion. The Establishment Clause insures that no state or federal government may pass laws that establish a church, aid a particular religion, or show preference to one religion over another. It also insures that the people of America may practice the religion of their choosing without being punished for their belief. It further protects the public from any tax burden levied for the purpose of supporting, teaching or practicing a religion.

Note: The "Establishment clause" referenced in many of these court cases, that you will soon be reading, refers to that part of the First Amendment to the Constitution which reads as follows: *"Congress shall make no law respecting **an establishment of religion**, or **prohibiting the free exercise thereof**; or abridging the freedom of speech, or the press or the right of the people peaceably to assemble, and to petition the Government for a redress of grievances."* So, the argument has to do with the first sentence of the First Amendment regarding the "establishment of a religion" or prohibiting the free exercise thereof.

The decision in the above case did not directly attack the right of religious education; however, the dissent by several of the Justices, opened the door for future such attacks on education. In his dissent in the *Everson* case, Justice Jackson, stated that public schools were designed to be secular and remain neutral in regard to religion or denomination. *"The assumption is that after the individual has been instructed in worldly wisdom he will be better fitted to choose his own religion."* Also, Justice Jackson stated *"religious teachings cannot be a private affair when the state seeks to impose regulations which infringe directly and the public affair when it comes to taxing citizens of one faith to aid another or those of no faith at all."*

Although the dessenting opinions in Court-rendered decisions are not binding, they are an indication of the feeling of certain members of the Court toward the subject matter and maybe considered by future judges in similar situations.

The attack on religious education actually began a year later in ***People of the State of Illinois, ex. rel. McCollum v. Board of Education of School District #71, Champagne County, Illinois***,[44] which was heard by the same court. This case involved the Champagne Council on Religious Education formed in 1940 by members of the Jewish, Catholic and Protestant faiths. Their purpose was to provide religious instruction classes to public school children in grades 4 through 9. The Champagne Council was given permission by the school board of Champagne County to offer weekly classes for 30 to 45 minute intervals for children of the Jewish, Catholic or Protestant faiths and would solely pay for any costs associated with conducting the classes. Each religious group held a class separate from each other, where participation in a religious class was subject to the express written consent of the parents requesting permission of attendance by their child. Once the children had permission to attend the classes, they would leave their regular classroom to attend the religious classes held on school grounds. Students, who elected not to participate in the religious instructions, were required to continue with their regular teachings.

Vashti McCollum sued the Board of Education, alleging a violation of the First (religious freedom) and Fourteenth (state's rights) Amendments requesting that the Court order the school board adopt and enforce rules and regulations prohibiting of all religious education in public schools in Champagne and public school houses and buildings in the said district.

The main issue in this case was, *"Does the use of public school facilities by religious organizations for the purposes of conducting religious instruction to school children, who elect to participate voluntarily, violate the First Amendment of the Constitution?"*

The Court held that, YES, it is unconstitutional to use public school facilities to conduct religious instruction classes for school children. The Court reasoned that the use of tax established and tax supported property for religious instruction aids religious groups spread their faith and serves in direct conflict with the Establishment Clause of the First Amendment which states that neither the state or the Federal Government may establish a church nor can they pass any laws which aid one religion, or all religions or show preference to any religion. The use of tax supported facilities along with the close working relationship between the school authorities and the religious council, in this case, also served as a way for children to become released from their legally imposed duty to receive secular education.

In the *Everson case*, the Supreme Court of the United States interpreted the First Amendment Establishment Clause to have drawn very distinct separation between church and state, that separation **"must be kept high and impenetrable."**[45] *(Remember these words as they will be used in many court cases!!)* The use of tax established and tax supported property for religious instruction aids religious groups to spread their faith. They serve in direct conflict of the Establishment clause which states that neither the state nor Federal Government may not establish a church nor can they pass laws which aid one religion, all religions or show preference to any religion. The use of tax supported facilities along with the close working relationship between the school authorities and religious council also serves as a way for children to become released from their legally imposed duty to receive non-religious education. The Court further held that there was no separation of church and state when the state mandates that all children must attend school and then allows the dissemination of religious instruction during the school day.

Four years later, in 1952 the United States Supreme Court in ***Zorach v. Clauson***,[46] the constitutionality of students receiving religious instruction during the school day was upheld. However, this case was a major departure from historical precedent in that the Court ruled the instruction must occur off campus. The basic facts in ***Zorach v. Clauson*** were that New York City schools participated in a released time program, where children, whose parents signed written permission, may leave the school campus early to participate in religious classes offered by the children's chosen denomination. The religious instructors report back to the school who was or was not in attendance as indicated. Although the classrooms were not on school campus, and they were not taught by any school employees; Zorach argued that the practices of New York City were not different than those of the McCollum case above, because the school still had major *"weight and influence"* on a program for religious instruction. The public school teachers were still required to have a close knit relationship with the leaders of the religious community. The teachers were responsible for keeping up with the children and reporting back.

The issue, in this case, was: *If the participation was in a "released time" program, is the state prohibiting the free exercise of religion or has it made a law respecting an establishment of religion within the meaning of the First Amendment?*

The Court said NO, the public schools were not participating in any promotion of religion, but were merely accommodating student's schedules so that they might be able to attend the religious programs of their choice.

The Court did say: *"the First Amendment, however, does not say that in every and all respects there shall be a separation of church and state."* Rather, it studiously defines the manner, the specific ways, in which there shall be no concert or union or dependency one on the other. That is the common sense of the matter. Otherwise, the state and religion would be alien to each other hostile, suspicious, and even unfriendly. Churches could not be required to pay property taxes. Municipalities would not be permitted to render police or fire protection to religious groups. Policemen, who helped citizens into their places of worship, would violate the Constitution. These and all other references to the Almighty running through our laws, are public rituals and our ceremonies would be flouting the First Amendment. Other examples include: prayers in our legislative halls appealing to the Almighty, and, any messages of the Chief Executive such as proclamations making Thanksgiving Day a holiday, and *"So Help Me God"* in our courtroom oaths. A fastidious Atheist or Agnostic could even object to the supplication with which the Court opens each session; **"God Save the United States and this Honorable Court."**[47]

So, in this case, the Court concluded that the argument for the separation of Church and state did not apply to student religious instruction during school hours… *"Unless separation of Church and state means that the public institutions can make no adjustments of their schedules to accommodate the religious needs of the people. We cannot read into the Bill of Rights such a philosophy of hostility toward religion."*[48]

With these cases and other similar cases heard by courts throughout the country, we are beginning to see a change in the philosophy and thought processes of the judiciary.

The plot thickens.

Ten years after the *Zorach* case, the Court had a change of justices. The new Court not only ceased to strike down voluntary religious activities for students, it actually upheld them. The Court retreated significantly from its inflexible concept of separation introduced in *Everson* and *Zorach*. In **Engle v. Vitale**,[49] the new Court took the philosophy from Charles Hughes, Chief Justice of the Supreme Court from 1930-1941, who declared **"We are under a Constitution, but the Constitution is what the judges say it is."**[50] Also, the Court recognized the words of the Chief Justice of the Supreme Court Earl Warren who stated, *"the Constitutional Amendment must draw its meaning from the evolving standards of decency that mark the progress of a maturing society."*[51]

During this Court's tenure, the Court indeed became a powerful social force striking down numerous long standing historical practices while proudly acknowledging that it was doing so without precedent.[52] **In other words, the Court publically announced that it had finally arrived at its fully evolutionary state no longer being bound by history or Court precedent.**

Several years later in **Walsh v. Tax Commissioner of New York, (1970)** the Court addressed the constitutionality of tax exemption for churches. In this case, the owner of real estate property in New York brought suit challenging the constitutionality of a state tax exemption law. The suit sought an injunction to prevent the City of New York Tax Commissioner from granting property tax exemptions to religious organizations for religious purposes and/or religious worship. The petitioner contended that he was being forced to make a contribution to religious bodies because the church property was exempted from paying property tax.

The issue to be decided by the Court was *"does a state law exempting religious organizations, which own property used for religious purposes, from paying property tax violate the religious clauses of the First Amend-*

ment?"

The Court held that NO, the law was not unconstitutional as an attempt to establish, sponsor or support religion or even as an interference with the free exercise of religion.

The Founders respected other religions; however, they knew they were purporting pure pluralism (a condition of society where numerous religious groups coexist with the country) and did not intend that the First Amendment do so. Although the Court's decision, in this case, was favorable in the sense that tax exemptions for churches were preserved. The ruling demonstrated a major inconsistency by the court. It upheld tax exemption because of their historical precedent.

Chief Justice Berger claims that the New York law does not serve to establish a religion but is rather *"sparing the exercise of religion from the burden of property taxation levied upon private property institutions."* Further, Justice Berger states that churches vary substantially in their good works for the public. It would not serve the public for the government to evaluate the worth and centers of these church-sponsored social welfare programs to determine the eligibility of exemption. Such evaluations would only promote the type of church-state involvements that the Constitution seeks to avoid. The exemption of property tax by the church serves to keep the entanglement of the government and the church minimized.[53]

Chapter 5

School Prayer

Prayer has always played a major role in our lives. The pilgrims prayed, the Constitutional Congress prayed, the various courts prayed; and, we pray before sporting events that no one will get injured, etc. However, since the 1960's the Courts have ruled that prayers in the public are unconstitutional, which totally reversed a 200 year tradition of encouraging prayers. That being said as a background; in the US Supreme Court case of **Engle v. Vitale**[54] the issue for the Court to decide was *"does state law and school district regulation ordering prayer to be recited in school violate the Establishment Clause of the First Amendment which is applicable to all states under the Fourteenth Amendment?"*

In a total reversal of previous cases and Court holdings, the Court here held YES, the practice adopted by the state of New York is *"wholly inconsistent with the Establishment Clause."* This is the famous case in which school prayers were removed by the United States Supreme Court. The rationale of this Supreme Court, which **cited no precedence or previous case law** to support their position, ruled there was no doubt that the implication as prescribed through this prayer does amount to a religious nature.

The religious nature of prayer itself was recognized by Thomas Jefferson and has been recognized by the Supreme Court of the United States, theological writers, state courts and administrative offices and even the Commissioner of Education for the State of New York. According to the Supreme Court, in this case, the use of prayer in the public school system breaches the Constitutional law of separation between church and state. In the most minimal capacity, the Establishment Clause of the United States Constitution expresses the notion that government has no business whatsoever composing official prayers for any group or reciting of official prayers as part of any government sponsored program. In fact, the very principle on which the Establishment Clause was created is the same on which America was founded. The Court's majority decision stated that: *"The Colonists sought to leave England to flee the imposition of government composed prayer and government composed regulations."*

Continuing, the Courts went on to say *"as well, to say that the government is acting hostile or against religion if they do not allow such activity to take place in schools and also wholly inconsistent with these principles, for the history of man is inseparable from the history of religion.*[55] *It is the need for man to worship as he pleases that brings forth the reasons that justify the separation between church and state. They merely fear that the governments of the past that shackle men's tongues to make them speak only the religious thoughts that government wanted them to speak and to pray only to the god that government wanted them to pray to. It is neither sacrilegious nor antireligious to say that each separate government in this country should stay out of the business of writing or sanctioning official prayers and leave that purely to religious function to the people themselves and to those people who choose to look for religious guidance."*[56] The real issue in this case, as the Court acknowledged, was simply the presence of prayer in the public school system.

It is obvious that this ruling was a direct attack on all types of prayers as shown by all cases since the *Engle* decision and has referred to the *Engle* case as a precedence, even though the *Engle* case sited **no previous court precedences.**

Why did it fail to cite precedent cases? Simply, there were none which could support its decision. For 170 years following ratification of the Constitution and the Bill of Rights, no court has ever struck down any prayer in any form in any location. Lacking precedent, the Court simply alleged a widespread public support, that is, *"since everybody"* knew that public school prayer was wrong, the Court cited a need to cite no precedence.

In 1931, the United States Congress adopted the "Star Spangled Banner" as the National Anthem. Within the "Star Spangled Banner" are

the following verses:
> "Blessed with victory and peace, may the Heaven rescued land
> Praise the power that hath made and preserved us a nation!
> Then conquer we must, when our cause it is just,
> And this be our motto "In God is our trust.""

In 1954, Congress added the phrase to the Pledge of Allegiance to the Flag so that it now contains the words **"One nation under God, indivisible, with liberty and justice for all"**. Are you also aware that since 1865 the words **"In God We Trust"** have been impressed on our coins? *(Although there is a current movement underway to remove those words from our currency!!!)*

In its decision, the Engle Court claimed that to allow this voluntary prayer was to establish an "official state religion". This statement was strenuously objected to by Justice Stewart who said: *"with all respects, I think the Court has misapplied a great Constitutional principle. I cannot see how an official religion is established by letting those who want to say a prayer say it. On the contrary, I think that to deny the wish of these school children to join in reciting this prayer is to deny them the opportunity of sharing in the spiritual heritage of our nation…for we deal here not with the establishment of a state church which, which would, of course, be constitutionally impermissible, but whether the school children who want to begin their day by joining in prayer must be prohibited from doing so."*[57]

Perhaps, the most serious and long lasting effect of the *Engle* case was the Court's decision to transform the First Amendment prohibition against the government establishing a traditional church into one prohibiting a voluntary religious activity by the students.

A year later, the Supreme Court again addressed a similar issue in the case of **Abington v. Schempp**.[58] That is actually a case where two companion cases with similar issues were decided together, because both cases involved state action requiring each school day begin with Bible readings.

The first case, **Abington v. Schempp**, takes place in the state of Pennsylvania where the legislature enacted a law requiring ten Bible verses to be read without commentary at the beginning of each school day. Everyday between 8:15 and 8:30 at Abington Senior High School, these exercises were conducted in conformity with the law at the high school, while supervised by a teacher. One student was chosen or volunteered to read the Bible verses of his or her choosing from whichever Bible version he or she chose. The scriptures were then read over an intercommunication system that was broadcast into each classroom followed by the Lord's Prayer wherein all students were asked to stand and join in the prayer, and the Flag salute finished with school announcements. Students were not compelled to join in the prayer. They could choose merely not participate or to leave the room. Over the time the exercise had been practiced, students had chosen a variety of scripture from which to read including the King James Version, the Douay Version, the Revised Standard Version or Jewish Holy Scriptures. The school board supplied the teachers with the King James Version but any version was authorized. There were no prefatory statements made during the exercise, no comments, no explanations, and the exercises were conducted to conform according to the state statute.

As a result of this activity, a lawsuit was filed by a Unitarian family alleging a violation of the First and Fourteenth Amendments. (Remember the First Amendment says in part: *"Congress shall make no law respecting an establishment of religion, or prohibiting the free exercise thereof;..."* and the Fourteenth Amendment states in part: *"...No state shall make or enforce any law which shall abridge the privileges or immunities of citizens of the United States; nor shall any State deprive any person of life, liberty, or property, without due process of law;... ."*) They sought to enjoin the state law, as well as, to stop the school district's Superintendent and other officers from continuing the exercises in the school where their children attended. The parents alleged that they contemplated having their children removed from the classroom while the exercises were being conducted; but, due to fear of harassment by teachers and classmates, the parents chose not to take such action.

The second case, heard at the same time, was **Murray v. Curlett**. This took place in Baltimore where the school board had adopted a rule similar to the *Schempp* case *(the "Murray" here is the famous Madeline Murray O'Hare)*. In the Murray case, the state of Maryland permitted school boards to adopt rules where a school day would be started with a reading, without comment, of a chapter in the Holy Bible and/or use of the Lord's

Prayer. Madeline Murray and her 13 year old son *(who interestingly enough later became a preacher!),* who were both proclaimed Atheists, attempted to have the school board rescind the rule. When the school board refused, Murray filed suit to force its rescission. The rule by the state of Maryland, like the one in Pennsylvania, included a provision that allowed the parents to request their child be exempt from the exercise which Murray did. However, Murray petitioned that her rights as an Atheist were being violated.

The Court had to decide the issue *"is it unconstitutional to allow the reading of the Bible and pray every morning as part of the public school day?"*

The Court, in both cases, held that it **was unconstitutional** under the Establishment Clause. The rationale of the Court was that "the First Amendment free exercise and establishment clauses are applicable to the states through the Fourteenth Amendment. And second, the Court has long held that the Establishment Clause, has not merely banned the government from showing preference for one religion to another, it uprooted all such relationships. In its rationale, the Court relied on the *Everson* case where they concluded that the First Amendment's scope was designed to forever suppress the establishment of religion or the prohibition of the free exercise thereof." In *Everson*, the Court also held that the First Amendment *"required the state to be neutral in its relation with groups of religious believers and nonbelievers; it does not require the state to be their adversary. State power is no more to be used so as to handicap religions than it is to favor them."*

The Court noted in these cases that, even though the schools' secular mission is *"the promotion of moral values, the contradiction to the materialistic trends of our times, the perpetuation of our institutions and the teaching of literature,"* the fact that these goals are attempted through the reading of the Holy Bible without comment followed by prayer do not support the school's claim that *"the Bible is here used either as an instrument or for non-religious moral inspiration or as a reference for the teaching of secular subjects."*

I feel that it is important to note here that the Court makes a huge distinction in this case between religious exercises, the teaching of the Bible for religious purposes, and the teaching of the Bible for secular purposes. The Court notes that it might well be said that *"one's education is not complete without a study of comparative religion or the history of religion in its relation to the advancement of civilization. It certainly may be said that the Bible is worthy of study for its literary and historic qualities. Nothing that we have said here indicates that such study of the Bible or of religion, when presented objectively as part of a secular program of education may not be effective consistently with the First Amendment. But the exercises here do not fall into those categories. They are religious exercises, required by the states in violation of the command of the First Amendment that the government maintain strict neutrality, neither aiding or opposing religion."*[59]

Like the New York prayer, this seemed to be a relatively innocent activity. It was voluntary; it was student led; no additional instruction or comments were permitted. Yet, today's civil libertarians portray this as a coercion case---so much so, they claim, that Edward Schempp thought himself forced to file a suit to relieve his children of this coercion. However, the facts of the case disprove this assertion:

Roger and Donna, two of the Schempp children, testified that they had never protested to their teachers or other persons of authority in the school system concerning the practices of which they now complain (in this lawsuit). In fact, on occasion, Donna herself had volunteered to read the Bible.[60]

Furthermore, so non-coercive was the policy that, while the other children were reading the Bible, one of the Schempp children had been permitted to read the Koran. The facts in the case clearly established that there was no coercion. It is interesting to note; however, when this case finally reached the United States Supreme Court, these facts were permitted in the District Court but were totally ignored by the Supreme Court!

In a very strong dissent, Justice Stewart made two major contentions. First, the idea that the two clauses of the First Amendment, the Establishment Clause and the Free Exercise Clause, present one absolute concept of "separation of church and state" in which all cases will be measured against is a fallacy. For *"we err in the first place if we do not recognize, as a matter of history and as a matter of the imperative of our free society, that religion and government must necessarily interact in countless ways."*

Second, the two clauses irreconcilably conflict with each other. *"The two relevant clauses of the First Amendment cannot accurately be reflected in a sterile metaphor which by its very nature may distort rather than eliminate the problems involved in a particular case".*

Justice Stewart went on to say the First Amendment was meant to limit the Federal Government. It was an attempt to insure that Congress not only be powerless to establish a national church but would also limit interference with existing state establishments. It was interesting that in Justice Stewart's dissent, he took the position that to be neutral, those students, who wish to participate in a religious activity, must be allowed to do so. If they were prohibited from such activities, they were denied a Constitutional right of free exercise. The argument, that Atheist or Agnostic children's Constitutional right of free exercise is violated, is not a bad argument in support of neutrality, but rather a violation of the Constitution due to the Government showing preference to secularism of a religion.

Joseph Story, U.S. Supreme Court Justice and father of the "American Jurisprudence," said *"one of the beautiful boasts of our municipal jurisprudence is that Christianity is part of the common law...there never has been a period in which common law did not recognize Christianity as lying at its foundations. I verily believe Christianity is necessary to support civil society."*[61]

Nowhere can it be demonstrated that the Founders desired to secularize (remove religion) official society and *"create a complete separation of the spheres of religious activity and civil authority."* The Abingdon decision represented a further step in the devolution of the First Amendment by rewriting the intent of those who created the Constitution and Bill of Rights.

The Founder's opinion of the Bible and of its use in school was quite clear:

> *"The Bible itself is the common inheritance, not merely of Christianity, but of the world."* Joseph Story, United States Supreme Court Justice; father of American Jurisprudence.
>
> *"The Bible is the book worth more than all the other books that were ever printed".* Patrick Henry.[62]

"The Bible is the best of all books, for it is the Word of God and teaches us the way to be happy in this world and in the next. Continue, therefore, to read it and to regulate your life by its precepts." John Jay, original Chief Justice of the United States Supreme Court.[63]

Not only did the Court disregard these stated beliefs of the Founding Fathers; the Court also asserted: *"The First Amendment's purpose was not to strike merely at this official establishment of a single sect...it was to create a complete and permanent separation of the spheres of religious activity and civil authority."*[64] This completely reverses the Founder's intent, because their purpose for the First Amendment was to *"strike at the official establishment of a single religion"* and definitely was not to completely and permanently separate their religious and civil lives.

In the two landmark decisions, *Engel* (1962) and *Schempp* (1963), the US Supreme Court established what is now the current prohibition on state-sponsored prayer in schools. While the *Engel* decision held that the encouragement of an official state-school prayer stood in violation of the First Amendment's Establishment Clause, *Schempp* held that Bible readings and other (state) school-sponsored religious activities were prohibited. Following these two cases came the Court's decision in *Lemon v. Kurtzman* (1971), a ruling that established the Lemon test for religious activities within schools. The Lemon test states that in order to be constitutional under the Establishment Clause of the First Amendment any practice sponsored within state run schools (or other public, state sponsored activities) must adhere to the following three criteria:

1. Have a secular purpose;
2. Must neither advance nor inhibit religion; and
3. Must not result in an excessive entanglement between government and religion.

Reactions to *Engel* and *Abington* were widely negative, where many school districts and states have attempted to reestablish school-sponsored prayer in different forms since 1962. Since the 1990s, controversy in the courts has tended to revolve around prayer at school-sponsored extracurricular activities. Examples can be seen where public prayers at graduation ceremonies and those conducted via public address system prior to high school games (at state school facilities before a school-gathered audience) were, respectively, ruled unconstitutional.

In 1985, the United States Supreme Court heard the case of **Wallace v. Jaffree**.[65] This Case involved an Alabama law which authorized a one minute period of silence at the beginning of each day for students to pray and meditate with voluntary prayer in schools. A resident brought the suit challenging the constitutionality of the law. Jaffree was the father of three minor children, who attended public schools in Mobile, Alabama. The Jaffrees brought action against the Mobile County School Board, various school officials, and specific teachers of these children alleging the violation of the Establishment Clause of the First Amendment. He alleged that two of his children had been subjected to religious indoctrination in fear that they would be ostracized by other classmates if they did not participate. He also alleged that he had made repeated attempts to stop the religious practices but was unsuccessful.

In this case, the constitutionality of three Alabama laws was being questioned. The first law provided that in all public schools there would be a one minute period of silence for *"meditation or voluntary prayer."* The second law slightly extended the first providing that there would be a period of silence *"for meditation or voluntary prayer."* The third law gives authorization to teachers to lead willing students in a prescribed prayer to *"Almighty God...the Creator and Supreme Judge of the world."*

The issue was: *whether an Alabama law simply authorizing a period of silence, or was the law respecting the establishment of religion within the meaning of the First Amendment?*

The Supreme Court said, YES, that this was a state endorsement of prayer activities in school as is prohibited by the First Amendment.

The Court found that, "the legislative intent to return prayer to the public schools is, of course, quite different from merely protecting every student's right to engage in voluntary prayer during an appropriate moment of silence during the school day." Moreover, the Court held the law unconstitutional because "the addition for 'voluntary prayer' in the case that the state intended to characterize prayer as a favorite practice." Such an endorsement is not consistent with the established principle that government must pursue a course of complete neutrality toward religion. *"The Court must make a finding on the question of 'whether the government intends to convey a message of endorsement or disapproval of religion anytime the state speaks on a religious subject.'"* Here the clear answer to that question was that the state undoubtedly meant to convey a message to the public schools of state approval.

The Alabama State legislature, in this case, had simply **permitted** a voluntary, silent activity. The Court concluded that this was the equivalent of encouraging a religious activity, an impermissible establishment of religion. Interestingly, Alabama came under the provisions of the U.S. Territorial ordinance which had declared that: *"religion, morality and knowledge, being necessary to a good government and the happiness of mankind, schools and the means of education shall forever be encouraged."*[66] History shows that the Founders considered it proper for the government to promote religious activities. For example: John Jay, the original Chief Justice of the United States Supreme Court, stated, *"It is the duty of all wise, free, and virtuous governments to countenance and encourage virtue and religion."*[67]

Henry Laurens, President of the Continental Congress of the U.S. diplomats and selected as a delegate to the Constitutional Convention, stated, *"I had the honor of being one among many who framed that Constitution…in order effectually to accomplish these great ends, is incumbent upon us to begin wisely and to proceed in fear of God; it is especially the duty of those who bear rule to promote and encourage respect for God and virtue and to discountenance every degree of vice and immorality."*[68]

Since the Founders, who prohibited the establishment of religion, also encouraged religion, it is clear…contrary to this Court's assertion… that the Founders did not equate encouraging or endorsing religion as establishment of religion. One of the justices on this Court, Sandra Day O'Connor, concurred with the majority opinion and further addressed the issue concerning "a moment of silence" in the school systems. She started off by saying that 25 states have statutes allowing a moment of silence during the school day; and, that of these states, there are courts that have struck down laws regarding a moment of silence because they have found that the purpose and effect were to encourage prayer or religion. Justice O'Connor also stated that, when looking at the law, the Court would look to the intent of the law by examining several different things including legislative history. If the Court has found that the legislative history provides that the purpose was to promote prayer and to promote religion or that, in any way at any time, the state conveys a message that the children should use a moment of silence for prayer then it violates the First Amendment.

Note: It is almost as if Justice O'Connor was saying while it is clear that the First Amendment is meant only for the purpose of protecting people from the government and governmental interference of the free exercise of their religion, we don't agree with that and We, the Court, think that there should be a separation of church and state. Therefore We, the Court, and not the Framers of the Constitution are going to redefine your constitutional liberties and find a way to get around this law in order to place workable limits on YOUR constitutional rights. However, it would be way too obvious for our unconstitutional intrusiveness into your life if we attempted to place any limits on your free exercise within your home. Therefore, we are going to make sure that we place these limits on the places that we have control over, such as public schools, court houses and any other governmental entity. If you want to enjoy your right to a free education or your right to the judicial system you WILL leave your religion at the door and play by our rules!

Justice William Rehnquist consented in the ***Wallace v. Jaffree*** decision arguing that there is much evidence to suggest that the well accepted meaning of the Establishment Clause, at the time enacted, was that it forbade the establishment of a national religion and prohibited preference among religious sects or denominations. "The Establishment Clause did not require government neutrality between religion and irreligion nor did it prohibit the Federal Government from providing nondiscriminatory aid to religion. There is simply no historical foundation for the proposition that the Framers of the Constitution intended to build the "wall of separation" that was constitutionalized in the Everson Case." Continuing, Rehnquist said, "The Framers intended the Establishment Clause to prohibit the designation of any church as a "national" one.

"The Clause was also designed to stop the Federal Government asserting a preference for one religious denomination or sect over others. Given the *'incorporation'* of the Establishment clause as against the states, states are prohibited as well from establishing a religion or discrimination between denominations. As its history abundantly shows, however, nothing in the Establishment clause requires the Government to be strictly neutral between religion and irreligion, nor does that clause prohibit Congress or the states from pursuing legitimate secular ends through nondiscriminatory sectarian means."

In closing Justice Rehnquist noted *"it would come as much of a shock to those who drafted the Bill of Rights, as it will to a large number of thoughtful Americans today, to learn that the Constitution, as construed by the majority of the Court, prohibits the Alabama legislature from "endorsing" prayer. George Washington himself, at the request of the very Congress which passed the Bill of Rights, proclaimed a day of "public thanksgiving and prayer, to be observed by acknowledging with grateful hearts the many and single favors of Almighty God." History must judge whether it was "the father of his country in 1789 or a majority of the Court today which has strayed from the meaning of the Establishment Clause."*[69]

The matter of prayers by students in public school has been a major issue for many years since the *Jaffree* Case. Here are a few examples:

Shultz, the Medina Valley Independent School District (2011)
Angela Hildenbrand, the valedictorian of her class, wanted to say a prayer during her graduation ceremony from Medina Valley High School. A fellow student from an Agnostic family filed a suit to prevent Hildenbrand from praying. The Federal District Court judge issued an order prohibiting Hildenbrand from using the words like Lord, Jesus, in Jesus' name and Amen. The Fifth Circuit Court of Appeals reversed the ruling and allowed the prayer. On July 6, 2011, Hildenbrand gave her speech which included the prayer.

McComb v. Crehan (2009)[70] In this case, school officials at Foothills High School in Las Vegas, Nevada told valedictorian Brittany McComb that she could not mention God or Jesus in her valedictorian address. When McComb did so anyway, the school officials turned off her microphone.

McComb sued the school for violating her free speech rights with the Ninth Circuit Court of Appeals which found that the school did not violate her Constitutional rights.

Mellen v. Bunting (2003)[71] Here, two students brought suit challenging the practice of having a supper prayer at a military school in Virginia on the grounds that it violated the Establishment Clause. The Court struck down the practice and banned the prayers.

ACLU of New Jersey v. Black Horse Pike Regional Board of Education (1996)[72] In this matter, a lawsuit was filed challenging a school policy that permitted the graduating class a vote to determine if there would be student led prayer during the graduation ceremony. The Court struck down the policy, determining that it violated the Constitution and ordered the school to forbid the prayer.

Workman v. Greenwood Community School Corporation (2010)[73] Greenwood, Indiana Community School had a tradition that, if the senior class voted to approve, such a measure of allowing a non-denominational prayer during the graduation ceremony would be permitted. In September of 2009, the senior class voted to allow a prayer. Eric Workman, a student at Greenwood, filed a suit to challenge the constitutionality of the electoral process allowing the prayer. The Court issued an injunction stopping such prayer.

Griffith v. Butte School District #1 (2010)[74] Rene Griffith, the class valedictorian at Butte High School, was selected to give a speech at her graduation ceremony. There were no written guidelines for student speakers but were told that remarks had to be *"appropriate, in good taste and grammar should be relevant to the closing of their high school years."* After meeting with the speech coach, Griffith was told that she needed to change her speech to omit any reference to *"God"* or *"Christ"* to be allowed to speak. Griffith refused to change her original remarks and was not allowed to speak. Griffith complained to the Human Rights Bureau but was given a notice of dismissal. The District Court found in favor of the school; however, the Supreme Court of Montana found that the school had violated Griffith's right to free speech but not her right to free exercise of religion.

These are very typical of the many cases involving prayer at schools and the school boards that are prohibiting prayers for fear of law suits and intimidation of municipalities and school boards by the ACLU, Freedom From Religion Foundation and others. It is just easier to cave in rather than fight, because of the prohibitive expense of defending the school prayer.

The United States Supreme Court: A Political and Legal Analysis discussed the results of a 1991 survey, stating that: *"The Court's school prayer decisions were, and still are, deeply unpopular with the public, many politicians and most religions organizations. Indeed, in a country where 95 per cent of the population believe in God and some 60 per cent belong to a religious organization, it comes as no surprise to learn that in a 1991 opinion poll, 78 per cent of Americans support the reintroduction of school prayer."* As a result of public support for school prayer in the United States, The Oxford Companion to the Supreme Court of the United States reports that *"The public's support for school prayer was translated by various state legislatures into statutes aiding religious schools and practices."*

One of the best emails that has been shared on the internet recently is this one:

"After being interviewed by the school administration, the prospective teacher said: 'Let me see if I have this right?

'You want me to go into that room with all those kids, correct their disruptive behavior, observe them for signs of abuse, monitor their dress habits, censor their T Shirt messages, and instill in them a love for learning.

'You want me to check their backpacks for weapons, wage war on drugs and sexually transmitted diseases, and raise their sense of self-esteem and personal pride.

'You want me to teach them patriotism and good citizenship, sportsmanship and fair play, and how to register to vote, balance a check book, and apply for a job.

'You want me to check their heads for lice, recognize signs of antisocial behavior, and make sure that they all pass the final exams.

'You also want me to provide them with an equal education regardless of handicaps, and communicate regularly with their parents in English, Spanish or any other language, by letter, telephone, newsletter and report card.

' You want me to do all this with a piece of chalk, a blackboard, a bulletin board, a few books, a big smile, and a start salary that qualifies me for

food stamps and EBT's.

'You want me to do all this, then you tell me…I CAN'T PRAY!!!!"
That about says it all!!!

Chapter 6

Ten Commandment Removal

The basic foundation of the Constitution and the majority of laws of the United States are based upon the Ten Commandments which are in the Old Testament. Since we are not allowed to show them in public places or schools any more, we list them as follows:

1. **I am the Lord your God. You shall have no other gods before me.**
2. **You shall not worship any idol.**
3. **You shall not take the name of the Lord, your God, in vain.**
4. **Remember the Sabbath and keep it Holy.**
5. **Honor your father and mother.**
6. **You shall not kill (murder).**
7. **You shall not commit adultery.**
8. **You shall not steal.**
9. **You shall not give false testimony (lie).**
10. **You shall not covet** *(desire other's possession).*[75]

(Emphasis added.)

In 1946 a juvenile delinquent appeared before Judge Ruegemer in St. Cloud, Minnesota, because the youth had struck and seriously injured another man while driving an automobile. After ordering a background check, he found out that the youth came from a troubled home.

The judge decided to suspend the juvenile's sentence, provided that he learned and lived by the Ten Commandments and reported regularly to his probation officer. When the youth explained he didn't know what the Ten Commandments were, the judge then made arrangements for a pastor to teach him about them. From this experience Judge Ruegemer realized that American youth needed the moral guidance provided by the Ten Commandments. He then began a movement to place monuments displaying the Commandments in thousands of courtrooms, schools, and parks across the nation.

In 1980, the U.S. Supreme Court heard the case of **Stone v. Graham**[76] in which the issue was the passive display of the Ten Commandments on the walls of schools in Kentucky. The basic facts were that a copy of the Ten Commandments was posted on every public school classroom in the state of Kentucky by force of a state law. The law rested on the fact that most laws developed for western civilizations and the United States stemmed from that of the Ten Commandments. Petitioners filed action claiming that it was a violation of the establishment of the Free Exercise Clause of the First Amendment.

The issue to be determined by this case was: *Does the posting of the Ten Commandments in the classroom of the public schools violate the Establishment Clause of the Constitution?*

The Court held, YES, the Ten Commandments in public schools serve no secular legislative purpose and is unconstitutional.

The Ten Commandments had been posted in the schools because the Kentucky legislature believed it *"…beneficial to expose students to the historical code which had formed the basis of civil laws in the western world for over 2000 years. Reflective of this, at the bottom of each poster was printed "the secular application of the Ten Commandments as clearly seen in its adoption as the fundamental legal code of western civilization and the common law of the United States."*

When the Supreme Court heard the Kentucky legislature's assertion that the Ten Commandments had secular importance, the Court stated, *"the preeminent purpose for posting the Ten Commandments on school room walls is plainly religious in nature. The Ten Commandments are undeniable a sacred text in the Jewish and Christian faiths, and no legislative recitation of a supposed secular purpose can bind us to that fact."*[77]

In his interesting dissent, Justice Rehnquist makes the point that it is equally deniable to say that the Ten Commandments are a sacred text as it is to say that the *"Ten Commandments have had a significant impact on the development of secular legal codes of the western world."*[78] Justice Rehnquist also says that the Establishment Clause has not required that the public sector be insulated from all things which may have religious significance or origin. This Court recognized that religion has been closely identified with our history and government *(Abingdon school district)* and that the history of man is inseparable from the history of religion *(Engel v. Vitale)*. Kentucky has decided to make students aware of this fact by demonstrating the secular impact of the Ten Commandments.[79]

(I wonder if the Court had forgotten that depictions of the Ten Commandments appear in two different locations inside the Supreme Court building in Washington when considering the Court's claim that the purpose for posting the Ten Commandments was purely religious in nature.) In addition, interestingly enough, over the head of the Supreme Court building there is a huge engraving of Moses with the Ten Commandments in his hands. The inscription under Moses states, "Justice the guardian of liberty." Our founders have laid in stone a truth that reproves those who sit in the Supreme Court chambers this day. Chief Justice Warren Berger noted in **Lynch v. Donnelly**, *"The very chamber in which all arguments in this case were heard is decorated with a notable and prominent---not seasonal---symbol of religion: Moses with the Ten Commandments."*[80] The position that the Court had also forgotten is that it is often easier to find the Ten Commandments displayed in government rather than in religious structures and that our civil prohibitions against theft, murder, perjury (lying in court), etc. are drawn straight from the Ten Commandments.

It is also interesting that, in the *Stone* case, the U.S. Supreme Court completely ignored the facts which led both the Kentucky legislature and the Federal District Court to acknowledge the secular *(non-religious)* importance of the Ten Commandments. It is amazing because the Court claims that the Ten Commandments lacked secular purpose, was the Court's complaint of what would occur if students were to view the Ten Commandments:

"If the posted copies of the Ten Commandments are to have any affect at all, it would be to induce the school children to read, meditate upon and perhaps venerate and obey the Commandments."[81]

The Founding Fathers must be rolling over in their graves after this decision. For example, John Witherspoon, a signer of the Declaration of Independence, stated **"the Ten Commandments...are the sum of all moral law."**[82]

"The opinion that human reason left without constant control of Divine laws and Commandments will...give duration to a popular government be as unlikely as the most extravagant idea to enter the head of a maniac. Where will you find any code of laws among civilized men in which the commands and prohibitions are not founded on Christian principles? I need not specify the prohibition of murder, robbery, theft and trespass." Noah Webster (1836).[83]

It is very clear that the prominent Founders of the Constitution and of the country say that the Ten Commandments, and the religious codes in general, are the foundation of American Civil Law. In fact, the belief was clear that public inherence to the religious principles was the greatest source of security for civil government.

Noah Webster said it perhaps best, *"All the miseries and evils which men suffer from vice, crime, ambition, injustice, oppression, slavery and war, preceding from their despising or neglecting the precepts contained in the Bible."*[84]

The Supreme Court declared this case unconstitutional...the very embodiment of a system which the Founders had embraced as the basis of our civilized society. The Court's decision in this case, not only struck down a passive non-coercive display, but also reflected the hostility which has become characteristic of the Court's decisions on these issues.

Chapter 7

Scholarships/Freedom Of Speech In Schools

Not only have attacks been made on schools and teachers, but the attacks on students and their activities, events, and use of scholarships are now coming under attack.

In 2004, Josh Davey, received a Promise Scholarship. This was awarded to academically gifted students with post secondary education expenses, to use at any college in the state. When he decided to pursue a double major in pastoral ministries and business management administration, he was told that he could use the scholarship for any major unless he was devoted to becoming a pastor. In a lawsuit, **Locke v. Davey**, (2004)[85] the United States Supreme Court ruled his scholarship could be withdrawn.

Because the public school system was in a "crisis of magnitude," Ohio enacted a voucher program in 2002 where families were given voucher funds to use toward the school of their choice. Many families elected to use their vouchers for religious schools. As a result, a lawsuit was filed to challenge the program, claiming it was unconstitutional because parents were allowed to choose religious over secular schools. The Supreme Court held that the program was neutral and was not a violation of the Establishment Clause.

Pennsylvania passed the Pennsylvania Home Education law in 1988. It is the most restrictive home school law in the United States requiring that families submit a teaching log, a portfolio of the child's work for review, and meet the requirements for the minimum number of days and hours in certain subjects. Six home school families sued to protect their right to educate their children after being subjected to truancy proceedings and social service investigations. The Federal District Court ruled that the law did not substantially burden the parents.

A teacher was made to remove religious materials from his classroom, including a picture of George Washington praying, an article showing religious differences of political candidates, and an article dealing with missionary activities of a student. The teacher brought suit against the school district. He argued that he was protected by the First Amendment Freedom of Speech and that the documents were displayed as history of the country. After a series of judgments against him, the Appellate Court finally ruled that the teacher was not protected by the First Amendment and thus had to remove all the religious materials.[86]

A biology teacher was prohibited from discussing religious matters with students while on the school campus even if the discussion occurred outside the class time and was student initiated. A lawsuit was filed to protect his constitutionally protected free speech and equal protection rights; but, the Court dismissed the complaint finding the school district's interest in avoiding an unlikely constitutional violation trumped the teacher's rights.[87]

The Maine state law required free public education for children through the 12th grade. The town of Minot had schooling through the 8th grade and either contracted to send these students elsewhere for high school or provided the parents with funding for school. Despite the fact that the state had authority to approve payments to alternative schools, a Minot family was denied access to public funding for their child's tuition to a Catholic high school. The family brought suit against the Maine Department of Education. The Court held that the state does not have to provide tuition for religious sectarian education. ***Eulitt v the Maine Department of Education (March 9, 2004)***[88]

LaRue v. The Colorado Board of Education (2011)[89] A Colorado state court permanently enjoined the Douglass County Colorado Board of Education voucher program that allowed students to enroll in the County's public schools, to use 75% of per student funding to attend private schools, including religiously affiliated schools. The Court held that the program violated many of the religious provisions of the Colorado Constitution, which it recognized as more restrictive than the religion clauses of the United States Constitution.

Free Speech in the School House

It is well established that students have First Amendment, Freedom of Speech, and rights in public schools.[90] Because public schools are places dedicated to learning, however, courts apply students' rights differently than in other contexts. In ***Santa Fe Independent School District v Doe (2000)***[91], the Supreme Court said: "There is a crucial difference between government speech endorsing religion, which the Establishment Clause forbids, and private speech endorsing religion, which the Free Speech and Free Exercise Clauses protect." According to the government publication, *Guidance on Constitutionally Protected Prayer in Public Elementary and Secondary Schools,*[92] public schools must treat religious expression the same way they treat similar non-religious expression; but, often the courts don't follow those guidelines.

In 1987, a suit was filed to challenge Louisiana's Creationism Act. The Creationism Act provided that if evolution is taught in public schools, Creationism Science must also be taught; and, if Creation Science is taught then Evolution must also be taught. The suit sought to strike down the Act as a violation of the Establishment Clause. In ***Edwards v. Aguillard (1987)***[93] the Supreme Court agreed striking down the law.

Lopez v. Candaele, (2010)[94] Jonathan Lopez, a student at Los Angeles City College, gave a speech about his faith and his traditional views of marriage. Lopez' professor stopped the speech, refused to grade it, and threatened to have Lopez expelled. Lopez sued the professor, a dean of the school, and the school, for violating his First Amendment rights of free speech. The District Court sided with Lopez; however, the Ninth Circuit Court of Appeals held that Lopez did not have standing to sue, because the teacher's statements are not a credible threat of harm.

Busch v. Marple Newtown School District (2009)[95] Elementary school students in the Marple Newtown School District were asked to select their favorite book which their parents would then read to the class.

Donna Busch's son chose the Bible. Busch selected a few verses that she often read with her son and was careful to select a psalm, because it omitted references to Jesus Christ. Despite numerous other presentations about Hanukah, Passover, Christmas and Easter being permitted in the classroom; the school's principal refused to allow Busch's son to fully participate because "reading the Bible to the class would be against the law" by promoting religion. The Third Circuit Court of Appeals upheld the restriction.

Nurrev v. Whitehead (2009)[96] A California high school banned a student from playing an instrumental version of a religious song at his graduation ceremony. The student brought suit and the Ninth Circuit Court of Appeals held that this prohibition did not violate the student's free speech rights and upheld the school's decision.

Corder v. Louis Palmer School District (2009)[97] The class valedictorian, Erica Corder, made a short speech during her graduation in 2006. The official policy of the school for school speeches did not mention religion but prohibited any speech that "tends to create hostility or otherwise disrupts the orderly operation of the educational process." Corder gave a speech that referenced her personal faith. At the conclusion of the ceremony, a teacher took Corder to speak with a school official. The school official informed Corder that she would not receive her diploma until she made a public apology for her speech. She refused and brought suit against the school district. The Court of Appeals ruled in favor of the school district and against Corder.

Fleming v. Jefferson County School District (2002)[98] We all remember the Columbine High School shooting a couple of years ago in which a student killed several other students in the Columbine Colorado High School. Following the tragedy, Columbine High School hosted a tile painting project so that students could express themselves. Some students expressed themselves with religious symbols including one by a victim's sister who incorporated a small yellow cross in her tile design. After the tiles were posted, the school officials removed the religious symbols from the tile display. The parents of the young lady, whose brother was killed, filed a lawsuit to prevent the school officials from censoring the religious expression of the students. The Tenth Circuit Court of Appeals chose not to uphold the student's expression of rights, and, instead, validated the school's censorship of their tile project.

Furley v. Aledo Independent School District (2000)[99] This case involved a young lady named Catherine Furley, who was elected to give the invocation at her graduation ceremony. She was ordered by the school to submit any prayer to officials ahead of time. School officials then proceeded to edit, word by word, which words she could and could not pray. Catherine's parents filed a lawsuit against the school district to protect her right to pray without being edited by the government. The Fifth Circuit Court of Appeals ruled against her right to pray in her own words without government editing.

Settle v. Dickinson County School Board (1995)[100] A Tennessee ninth grader, Brittany Settle, selected "Jesus Christ" as the topic for her open research project; however, her teacher refused to approve her project and gave Brittany a zero for her grade. Her teacher did not permit her to submit another project. A lawsuit was filed by Brittany's parents to protect her free expression of rights; but, the Court refused to uphold Brittany's rights and ruled in favor of the school.

Denooyer v. Merinelli (1993)[101] When Kelli Denooyer was selected as her class VP of the week, she brought in a video of her singing a solo at a church to share with her class. The teacher refused to play the tape, for a variety of reasons, including her concern about the video tape's religious message. Kelli's parents filed a suit against the teacher, but the Sixth Circuit Court of Appeals upheld the censorship of the video.

Eder v. City of New York (2009) Melissa Eder, an art teacher at the East New York Family Academy, filed a suit claiming discrimination and retaliation. Eder, who was Jewish, asserted that her co-worker's practice of voluntarily forming prayer circles before meetings was unconstitutional. She claimed that this practice, including prayer which was offered before a holiday party, was unconstitutional and a violation of her rights. Following a hearing by the Court on the matter, the Court held that the faculty member's voluntary decision to engage in prayer before meetings at the holiday party was not a violation of Eder's rights.[102]

In 2006, a New York District Court had an interesting holding. The Mexico Academy High School of New York decided to remove any brick, if they contained any Christian message, which had been purchased and inscribed as part of a school fundraiser. After hearing the facts, the District Court held that removing the bricks with the Christian messages violated the First Amendment rights (Freedom of Speech) of the donors.[103]

Washegesic v. Bloomingdale Public Schools (1994)[104] A portrait of Jesus Christ hung in the hallway of a school, along with other portraits of famous individuals and, a former student filed suit against the school, asserting that the portrait was an Establishment Clause violation. The Court agreed and ordered the picture removed.

Duran v. Nitsche (1991)[105] A fifth grader, Dianna Duran, was a member of the academically talented program and was assigned an independent study project. She completed it on the topic, "Power of God", which was originally approved by her teacher. Her research included a survey of her classmate's religious beliefs and the assignment included presenting her project to the class. However, school officials intervened and prevented Dianna from successfully completing the project. Her parents filed a lawsuit to protect her First Amendment Freedom of Speech rights. But, the Court held that she had no such rights in the classroom.

These are just a few of the many cases of a similar nature with similar decisions. Significantly, the decision to remove the Bible from schools, just like the decision to ban voluntary prayer, was a reversal of all previous practice and rulings by the Court on that issue. The U.S. Supreme Court in the 60's was simply announcing yet another new position, in essence saying: ***"the majority of the nine of us on this court simply do not want the Bible in schools anymore!"***

Following those two landmark rulings in the 60's ***(Engle v Vitale and Abington v Schempp)***, courts continued to expand their new secular requirements to more areas. For example, in 1967 a Federal Court declared a four line nursery rhyme used by a kindergarten class to be unconstitutional. The Court acknowledged that the word *"God"* did not appear anywhere in the nursery rhyme; nevertheless, it was still unconstitutional.[106] Apparently, if someone were to hear the rhyme, he might ***think*** that it was talking about God, and that would be unconstitutional. This trend of hostility toward religious expression has continued in case, after case and year after year.

As previously discussed, by 1980 the Supreme Court even addressed whether students could continue voluntarily saying the Ten Commandments while at school. In the case of **Stone v. Graham**,[107] the Ten Commandments were acknowledged to be a passive display of just like any one of the many pictures at school. That is, a student might see a picture of George Washington or a field of flowers or the Ten Commandments or a Lighthouse on the seashore or student art work, etc. hanging on the wall. The Ten Commandments were not part of any curriculum. They were just passively hung on the wall like any other picture. You could look at them, if you wanted to, and if you didn't want to, you could just walk on by.

Nevertheless, the Supreme Court in its infinite wisdom(?) ruled that allowing students, even voluntarily, to see a passive copy of the Ten Commandments at school was unconstitutional. The Court stated: *"If posted copies of the Ten Commandments are to have any effect at all, it will be to induce the school children to read, meditate upon, perhaps to venerate and obey the Commandments…this is not a permissible state objective."*

Can you believe that? What logic! Students cannot see the Ten Commandments even if they want to, for they might obey "religious teachings" such as, "don't steal", or "don't kill", because it would be unconstitutional!

Do decisions of the 1960's, throwing God's principles out of schools, have any measurable statistical effect? You can answer that! When you were in school, do you recall any students or others entering the school and killing students? I doubt it.

George Washington warned of this particular action by the Supreme Court in his "farewell address" when he said: "let us with caution indulge in the supposition that morality can be maintained without religion. Whatever may be concluded to the influence of refined educational minds of peculiar structure (that is, on the impressionable minds of students), reason and experience both forbid us to expect that national morality, can prevail in exclusion of religious principles."[108] In that address, Washington forewarned that excluding religious principles from the education of students would result in a loss of morality. Statistics have confirmed the accuracy of his warning. Just look at the birth rates of unwed girls 15-19 since 1963 or the amount of sexually transmitted diseases between the age group

10-14. Particularly check out the violent crime and number of offenses that has skyrocketed since 1962, when the Supreme Court acted on the cases previously mentioned. Clearly, following the Court's 1960's decisions, moral measurements for students broke violently in the wrong direction..

The Founding Fathers understood that America could only prosper under God's blessings; and, therefore, refused to separate His principle from any aspect of public affairs. The Founders recognized that for God to bestow His blessings, His principles had to be honored and embraced. George Washington said, *"The propitious smiles of Heaven could never be expected on a nation that disregard the external rules of order and right which Heaven itself has ordained."*[109]

The very thought of disregarding what Washington identified as God's *"eternal rules of order and right"* was a fearful thought for the Founding Fathers. As Thomas Jefferson said: *"I tremble for my country when I reflect that God is just---that His justice cannot sleep forever."*[110]

Of course, the Founders reasoned that God would bless or oppose a nation based on the degree to which it embraced His policies. This makes sense, only if there is a God, only if God has established rights and wrongs, and if God responds to a nation on that basis. The Founders believed that these "ifs" were true, and stressed that God should be openly and publicly acknowledged throughout the public arena.

Chapter 8

Attacks On Teachers And School Administrators - *it just gets worse!*

Teachers and school administrators are constantly being attacked for their decisions and policies regarding any kind of religious discussion in schools. As you have already seen, school districts are quite often the target of lawsuits based upon religious principles. The problem with most school districts is that they are generally short of funds; are unable to defend a lawsuit, because it would put them in a serious financial condition. The way they often handle the situation is to simply bow down to a threat of suit and prohibit any religious activity or even discussions, in order to prevent the suit. Some schools do try to fight back, but the courts are so afraid of being reversed by an appeals court, that they will typically back the school systems' decisions, much to the detriment of the students and parents.

Here are a few lawsuits to illustrate my point.

John Doe 3 v. Elmbrook School District (2012)[111] In this matter, the Plaintiff sued the Elmbrook School District in Wisconsin claiming its practice of using a Christian church as the locale for the high school's annual graduation ceremony, violated the Establishment Clause of the First Amendment. The school did not have a location large enough to accommodate the crowds for the graduation ceremony. They used a Christian church as their location. The Seventh Circuit Court of Appeals held that holding a graduation in the church violated the Establishment Clause of the Constitution.

Adams v. Trustees of University of North Carolina-Wilmington[112]
In this case, a professor at the University of North Carolina Wilmington was denied a promotion based upon the religious and political views that he expressed in his newspaper column and in his speeches. The Fourth Circuit Court of Appeals held that the professor's speech was constitutionally protected as private speech.

Borden v. School District of the Township of East Brunswick[113]
Marcus Borden was the head football coach at East Brunswick High School and often engaged in silent acts of prayer such as bowing his head to say grace prior to eating or taking a knee with his team during locker room prayer. He filed a suit to declare that he was allowed to engage in this silent behavior despite the East Brunswick School District's policy prohibiting faculty participation in student initiated prayer. The Third Circuit Court of Appeals found that Borden's activities would lead a reasonable observer to conclude that Borden was endorsing religion.

Iowa State University banned students from exploring Biblical insights into Business Management.[114] Despite implementation by successful businesses, such as Hobby Lobby and Chick-Fil-A, the growing interest in spirituality's role in successful businesses, Iowa State University joined by the ACLU, derailed the plan for its students to examine Biblical insights into Business Management. After the course was first approved, 20 faculty members objected to the course purporting to be concerned about academic rigor and that for First Amendment purposes, it established a state religion. These students were not permitted to examine the Biblical insights into Business Management.

Roarke v. South Iron R-1 School District[115] For 30 years, South Iron Elementary School had permitted the Gideons to distribute Bibles to the students. A student sued, claiming that the distribution of Bibles in school violated the Establishment Clause. The Eighth Circuit Court of Appeals agreed and prohibited further distribution of Bibles.

The Christian Legal Society ("CLS") Chapter at Arizona State University College of Law, the Crow,[116] requires its members to agree with CLS's statement of faith. Arizona State University denied its CLS chapter from becoming an official student organization because requiring agreement with a statement of faith did not comply with the University's religious non discrimination policy. CLS filed a lawsuit and received a favorable settlement. Arizona State now allows religious student groups to limit membership to those who share their religious beliefs.

Harrison v. Gregoire (2002)[117] University of Washington and Eastern Washington University both enforce policies that barred students teaching at religious schools. The universities cited the "Blaine Amendment", which called for a strict separation of church and state. Caroline Harrison and Renee Penhallurick, teaching students at the universities, hoped to complete their student teaching at religious schools but were denied the opportunity. These students brought suit against the universities. As a result of the lawsuit, the State of Washington's policy now requires that universities can either allow or deny student teaching at private schools regardless of religious status. The University of Washington changed its policies allowing Harrison to teach at a Jesuit school. Eastern Washington University decided to prohibit student teaching at any private school.

Sometimes you win and sometimes you lose!

Chapter 9

Attacks Against Churches And Ministries

Since the earliest days of our country, there have been groups who oppose any type of religion or religious beliefs. As a result of these feelings and beliefs, there have been attacks on religion in general, the religious institutions (churches, synagogues, temples, etc.), and even the individuals who teach religion. People often forget that the first schools and colleges in the United States were formed and built by religious believers to teach people to read and understand the Bible to learn the values and history it contains. The problem today is many people of the United States have become so complacent that they really don't care about what is happening to the country, its people, or even why it is happening! The largest majority of ministers, priests, rabbis, and other teachers of religious beliefs are there to help the spiritual lives of the people and teach them the values of morality, so the world will be a better place. However, there have been, and are going to continue to be, attacks against churches and ministries.

Here are a few instances where that has occurred in recent years.

Hein v Freedom From Religion Foundation (2007)[118] The Freedom From Religion Foundation filed a lawsuit against the White House claiming the Establishment Clause bars faith based charities from receiving government funding. In a 5-4 decision, the United States Supreme Court ruled that an Atheist organization lacked tax payer standing to challenge a White House conference that informed both faith based and secular organizations about Federal funding for programs that helped the poor.

Mitchell v. Helms (2000)[119] Under the Education Consolidation and Improvement Act of 1981, government aid for materials and equipment was provided to public as well as private schools. A lawsuit was filed against the Act because it would allow private schools, which are religious schools in many cases, to receive a benefit. The Supreme Court held that this funding did not violate the Establishment Clause.

Opulent Life Church v. City of Holly Springs, MS (2012)[120] The Opulent Life Church in Holly Springs, MS had nearly outgrown its own present meeting place and needed to move to a larger facility. Once the church found a new property, it was discovered that the city would not grant a permit for the church to move into the new property without getting permission of 60% of all property owners within a quarter mile radius of the proposed site---a requirement that applied only to churches and to no other type of facility or business. The Opulent Life Church is suing the city of Holly Springs for violating the Constitution and the RLUIPA which is the Religious Land Use Institutionalized Person's Act. This prohibits zoning ordinances from discriminating against churches.

Centro Familiar Christiano Buenas Nuevas Christian Church v. City of Yuma (2011)[121] A church in Yuma, Arizona purchased an old department store to use as a new church building. Yuma required that the religious organizations receive a permit to use a building for religious purposes. The city denied the permit claiming that it wanted to convert the part of the city where the department store was located into an entertainment district and no bars, nightclubs or liquor stores could be within 300 feet of a church under the current law. The Ninth Circuit held that, under the RLUIPA, the city could not single out a church for discrimination in zoning restrictions.

Glassman v. Arlington County, VA (2010)[122] In 2004, First Baptist Church of Clarendon in Arlington County, VA proposed a plan to build a 10 story building on church property. The bottom two floors would be used as a church, and the upper eight floors would be used for apartments including some low to moderate rent apartments. Arlington County approved these plans and provided loans to finance the construction of the apartments. Glassman sued the County claiming that this involvement violated the Establishment Clause of the First Amendment. The Fourth Circuit Court of Appeals held that the County's involvement did not advance the First Baptist Church of Clarendon's faith. There was NO violation of the Establishment Clause.

Koniko v. Orange County (2008)[123] Alleging that Rabbi Joseph Koniko was in violation of local law prohibiting "operating a synagogue or any function relating to a synagogue and/or church services," he was ordered by the Orange County code enforcement officials to stop holding prayer meetings in his home. Rabbi Koniko was ordered to stop the prayer meetings or face daily fines totaling nearly $53,000; however, the Court of Appeals ruled that Koniko was within his rights under the Constitution to hold those meetings and that the ordinance was unconstitutional.

Petra Presbyterian Church v. Village of North Brook (2007)[124] Following a purchase of property by a church, the Village of North Brook, a suburb of Chicago, Illinois, changed the zoning ordinance to prevent churches from operating within its zone and obtained an injunction to prevent the church from meeting. The Court of Appeals held that the church failed to show that the altered zoning ordinance burdened the church's exercise of religion even though they had to meet elsewhere.

Grace United Methodist Church v. City of Cheyenne (2006)[125] The City of Cheyenne, Wyoming, denied a nonprofit church's request for a variance to operate a daycare in a residential area. The church sued the City of Cheyenne. The Court affirmed that the exercise of a daycare was not a sincere exercise of the church's religion, and that the city had properly denied the church's daycare request in the interest of the health, safety and welfare of citizens.

Amandola v. Town of Babylon (2001)[126] Romans Chapter 10 Ministries, Inc. had obtained a permit to use Babylon's town hall annex to hold worship services; but, when an angry resident called the city to complain about the facilities being used for church services, the town revoked the permit. The church filed a lawsuit to protect their right to access the community facilities and to end religious discrimination. The Second Circuit Court of Appeals held that the revocation of the permit violated the First Amendment.

Calvary Christian Center v. City of Fredericksburg, VA (2011)[127] The City of Fredericksburg, VA denied a local church's permit application to use its property to run a private school. The church brought suit against the city to allow the school; however, the Court dismissed the case for failure to state a claim because running a school is not a protected religious exercise under the Free Exercise Clause of the Constitution's First Amendment.

Family Life Church v. City of Elgin (2008)[128] H.E.L.P.S. a Christian homeless ministry operating out of a church building was told that the city required the church to obtain a building occupancy permit and zoning permission to keep the ministry open. The Elgin city manager informed them that a conditional use permit would also be necessary and told them that the chances of obtaining one from the city council were *"a million to one against it."* After the city drove the organization from Family Life Church, H.E.L.P.S. began ministering at a camp 20 minutes from outside the city on weekends and at other churches on their bus. The District Court held that the city's actions did not violate the First Amendment.

Barr v. City of Sinton (2009)[129] Pastor Barr's Christian organization, which provides housing and religious instruction to men who have been released from prison for misdemeanor offenses, was completely banned by the City of Sinton from existing anywhere within its city limits. In a landmark decision, the Texas Supreme Court applied the Texas Religious Freedom Restoration Act to rule in favor of Barr.

Cambodian Buddhist Society of Connecticut, Inc. v. Planning and Zoning Commission of the Town of Newtown (2008)[130] Pong Me and the Cambodian Buddhist Society of Connecticut purchased property in the city of Newtown, Connecticut on which they planned to build a Buddhist temple. The city's planning and zoning commission denied them a building permit and argued that the Asian architecture, potential noise and possible high volume of cars near the temple would disrupt the harmony of the surrounding neighborhood. Using a Connecticut religious freedom law, the society took the city to court. In 2008 the Connecticut State Supreme Court ruled in favor of the city banning the society from building its temple.

Sometimes lawyers get creative in religious suits trying new ways to influence the courts to remove religion from the public. Here is probably one of the more famous such examples where a person tried to get a city to tax religious institutions.

Waltz v. Tax Commission City of New York[131] This Supreme Court (the same basic justices that sat on the Court in the 1960's rendering anti-religious opinions such as removing prayers from schools, etc.) addressed the constitutionality of tax exemptions for churches. The basic facts in this case were that the owner of real estate property in New York brought suit challenging the constitutionality of a state tax exemption law. It sought to prevent the New York City Tax Commissioner from granting property tax exemption to religious organizations for religious properties used solely for religious worship by religious organizations. The petitioner, Waltz, contented that he was being forced to make a contribution to religious bodies because the church property was exempt from paying property taxes.

The question for the Court to decide was: *does a state law exempting religious organizations from paying property taxes on property owned by the organizations, violate the religious clauses of the First Amendment?*

Here, the Court said NO, the law is not unconstitutional as an attempt to establish, sponsor or support religion or as an interference with the free exercise of religion. Interestingly, the Court majority said, *"first, the legislative purpose of a property tax exemption is neither the advancement nor the inhibition of religion; is neither sponsorship nor hostility."*[132] The Court explained that the petitioner, Waltz, failed to realize that the exemption is not one strictly applied for religious purposes. The property tax exemption in New York, as well as most states, provides that all organizations that serve the community at large by moral or mental improvement, should not be hindered by paying property taxes when the income could be better applied to the community projects in which they foster.

Further, the property they use should not be subject to seizure for their inability to pay property taxes. Religious institutions are not the only organizations subject to such provisions determined by the Court. Continuing, the majority on the Court said, *"Other nonprofit organizations that are granted exemptions include hospitals, libraries, playgrounds, scientific, professional and other groups."*

In determining the effect that the law has, it could be argued that the tax exemptions create an indirect economic benefit; however, the government is in no way sponsoring church activities because it does not transfer any government revenue to the churches. The state, through this exemption, continued the Court, *"is making sure that in no way does the church support the state."* This case introduced a further step in the continued rewriting of the First Amendment when Justice William Douglas claimed that its purpose was to enhance non-religion and to promote pluralism (one which acknowledges no religion or system of belief above any other): *"one of the mandates of the First Amendment is to promote a viable pluralistic society and to keep government neutral, not only between sects, but also between believers and non believers."*[133]

There is no question that the Founding Fathers respected many major religions. However, the Founders respect for other religions should not be confused or misinterpreted as a promotion of pluralism---as stated by this statement from Benjamin Rush:

"Such is my feeling for every religion that reveals the attributes of the Deity, or a future state of rewards and punishments, that I had rather see the opinions of Confucius or Mohammed inculcated upon our youth, than to see them grow up in a wholly devoid system of religious principles. But the religion I mean to recommend in this place is that of the New Testament."[134]
(You will remember that Benjamin Rush was one of the original Founders and signators of the Declaration of Independence.)

Noah Webster, one of the founders and early educators in the United States said, *"the Christian religion, in its purity, is the basis or rather the source of all genuine freedom in government...and I am persuaded that no civil government of a republican form can exist and be durable in which the principles of that religion have not been a controlling influence."*[135]

Most of the Founding Fathers demonstrated their preference for Christianity and provided no evidence of any alleged *"mandate to promote a visible, pluralistic society".* The Founders did respect other religions; however, they neither promoted pluralism nor intended that the First Amendment do so either.

Although the Court's decision in this case was favorable, in the sense that tax exemptions for churches were preserved, the ruling demonstrated **a major inconsistency by the Court.** It upheld tax exemptions because of their historical precedent! The *Waltz* Case, despite its favorable ruling, had, by claiming its **intent** was to promote pluralism, introduced yet another new and different purpose in the First Amendment. For generations, the understanding of what constituted a *"religion"* was simple and strait forward: *"religion"* was defined as *"a belief in the being and perfections of God, in the revelation of His will to man, and man's obligation to obey His commands, in a state of reward and punishment, and in man's accountability to God."*[136] Interestingly, groups that did not acknowledge some type of Supreme Being were never considered to be religions. However, in the early 1960's, when the very liberal Supreme Court decided to reject the long standing meaning of the First Amendment, it also decided to reject the long standing meaning of *"religion."* Just as it wrote its own new First Amendment, the Court also wrote its own new definition for *"religion"* saying that whatever a person believes so strongly that it affected the way that he behaved was considered his religion.[137] As a consequence, many beliefs, creeds and philosophies that completely denied the existence of any Supreme Being suddenly became a religion!

For example, the courts now hold that Atheism is a religion.[138] Since Atheism is the essence of anti-religion, how can anti-religion be a religion? What are the religious beliefs of Atheists? Atheists devoutly believe that there should be no public religious expressions. So, the religion of Atheism is a religion of practicing no religious practice; that is, it is religiously practicing non-religion, and the courts officially consider it to be a First Amendment religion entitled to full religious protection. *Go figure that one!!!!*

If that belief wasn't farfetched enough, consider this: courts and government officials have also ruled that satanic and Wiccan groups are religions and that people may now give contributions to those groups and receive the same tax deductions as people who give to Christian churches or Jewish synagogues.[139]

It just gets more extreme! The Court also considered secular humanism to be a religion equivalent, under the law, to Christianity.[140] What is the primary purpose of the religion of secular humanism? It is the conviction that life revolves around man rather than God…it is a man centered philosophy that excludes God. The Church of Scientology, which began in the early 1950's, is now considered an official religion.[141] Its beliefs are simple: *"in Scientology, no one is asked to accept anything as belief or on faith. That which is true for you is what you have observed to be true."*[142] The truth in this *"religion"* is individually determined and measured...it is whatever an individual person picks and chooses to be true.

The beliefs of all these types of groups were protected by the First Amendment *"as free speech"* clause as well as its assembly clause (i.e. the right for persons to assemble and gather into groups of their choice) but NOT by its religion clauses. Those clauses existed to protect the truly religious. Now, as you can see, the Constitutional protection for the genuinely religious have been expanded to include every individual, even the non- and the anti- religious, thereby throwing out the true religious protections.

Today, there is obviously a double standard. The *"separation of church and state"* only means that Biblical principles must be kept out of the public, not the principles, beliefs or practices of other religions (or even so called religions). A clear demonstration of this fact, is that a California Federal Court ruled that it was not constitutional for public school students to say *"under God"* in the Pledge of Allegiance,[143] but it was constitutional for public schools to require a three week general indoctrination to the Islamic faith in which Junior-High School students...even those who are not Muslim...must pretend that they are Muslims. They must offer prayers to Allah, and they are further urged to take Islamic names and call each other by those names, wear Islamic garb, participate in Jihad games, and read the Koran during those three weeks. It is interesting that the Ninth Circuit Federal Court of Appeals did not think that requiring Islamic religious activities violated the so called "separation of church and state," but voluntarily saying "under God" in the Pledge of Allegiance did!

In short, *"separation of church and state,"* as it exists today, is not a teaching of the family values or even historical teaching. It is the war cry of the courts in the anti-Biblicists.

Chapter 10

Religious Group Discrimination

In the past, school districts around the country have been able to use church facilities for such things as graduation and other events when the school's facilities were simply too small to accommodate the crowds. Also, many church facilities have been used as school classrooms on a temporary basis when local rooms were not available. The reverse has also been true. Many churches have rented or used public school facilities, not being used by the schools, to hold religious or other meetings, when there was not room at the church. The resulting activities have resulted in law suits, the decisions of which have bounced both ways.

In the case of ***Widmar v. Vincent,***[144] the University of Missouri at Kansas City refused to allow a religious student group equal access to university facilities like other student sponsored groups. The students were forced to file a lawsuit in order to protect their rights to equal access and to stop the religious discrimination which was upheld by the United States Supreme Court.

Board of Education of the West Side Community Schools v. Mergens, (1990)[145] This was a case in which a school board refused to allow students to form an extracurricular Christian club claiming that such a club would violate the Establishment Clause of the Constitution. The lawsuit had to be filed to protect the Christian group from being unlawfully discriminated against by the school board. The United States Supreme Court upheld the discrimination charge, and the school board was forced to allow the students to form the club.

In 1993, a New York school board denied a church after hour access to a school to exhibit a film series about Christian family values because of a policy prohibiting use by any group for religious purposes. The school board had allowed other groups use of the facility in the past. A lawsuit, Lambs Chapel v. Center of Moriches Union Free School District, was filed to protect the church's right to have equal access to the school which again was upheld by the United States Supreme Court.[146]

A very interesting situation occurred in the State of Florida in late 1993, in which the Church of the Lukumi Babalu Aye sought to set up a church in Florida. The church practices Santeria, a religion that incorporates animal sacrifice into its religious practices. Upon hearing of the church's plan to develop a church in the city, the city council held an emergency meeting and passed ordinances to prevent the church from practicing the animal sacrifice, an essential part of the church's free exercise. The church brought suit against the city[147] to protect the church's right to free exercise. The Supreme Court ruled against the city and allowed the church to build within the City of Hialeah.

In 1995, the University of Virginia refused to provide funds to print a journal because of the journal's religious viewpoint. The student promoting the journal filed a lawsuit to challenge the fund's disbursement guidelines that discriminated against religious viewpoints. The Supreme Court held in **Rosenberger v. Rector and Visitors of the University of Virginia**[148] that providing funds to publish the journal would not violate the Establishment Clause; therefore, the school could not discriminate against the journal because of its religious viewpoint.

Good News Club v. Milford Central School (2001)[149] This case was decided by the United States Supreme Court in 2001. Here the Milford Central School denied the Good News Club's afterhours use of the school's facilities. A lawsuit was filed to protect the religious group's right to use the school's facilities, as other organizations were permitted to do, without being discriminated against. The Supreme Court held that this was not discrimination and allowed the Milford School Board to deny the use of the facilities.

Community House, Inc. v. City of Boise (2007) The City of Boise, Idaho, leased a homeless shelter to a nonprofit Christian organization which provided voluntary chapel services and other religious activities at the shelter. The city then barred religious activities from the shelter. The organization filed a lawsuit to protect its right to conduct religious activities at the shelter.[150] A Federal District Court prohibited the city from banning religious activities at the shelter; but, the Ninth Circuit Court of Appeals reversed saying that there should be no religious activities at the shelter even if participation is voluntary.

Four years later in the same city, the Inner Mountain Fair Housing Council and two individuals filed suit against Boise Rescue Mission Ministries. They alleged that the Mission was in violation of the Fair Housing Act, and by holding chapel services and requiring guests in the discipleship program to participate in religious programs, it engaged in religious discrimination. The District Court ruled in favor of the Mission, which was a homeless shelter that receives no government funding and provides free and voluntary services. Interestingly enough, the Ninth Circuit Court of Appeals agreed. *Figure that?*

The City of Albuquerque, New Mexico, prohibited Church on the Rock from showing a religious film at a senior center or passing out Bibles to people at the center. Church on the Rock sued to be able to show the film and distribute the Bibles. A Federal District Court found for the city; but, the Tenth Circuit Court of Appeals reversed, holding that the City of Albuquerque had engaged in an unconstitutional viewpoint discriminating against the church.[151]

The Freedom From Religion Foundation wrote a letter to the United States Air Force Academy complaining about its encouraging cadets to participate in the support of the Academy's Operation Christmas Child project. Operation Christmas Child is a charity that sends children Christmas presents along with a religious message. The Academy responded to the letter by no longer directly encouraging the project and only allowing the school chaplains to promote participation.[152]

The American Civil Liberties Union (ACLU) is, and has been for many years, very active in trying to prevent religious activities in public among their other activities. The ACLU attempted to force Harrison County, West Virginia, to discriminate against a religious festival in its grant distribution period. The County prosecuting attorney refused to discriminate, noting that the grant funding process was neutral toward religion.

In another instance, the ACLU sued Neptune High School in Neptune, New Jersey, because the school decided to continue with their seventy year tradition of holding its graduation ceremonies at the Great Auditorium of the Ocean Grove Camp Meeting Association, a Methodist organization. The school and the ACLU settled with the school agreeing to cover any religious symbols in the Great Auditorium.

In Irving, Texas, the Irving Independent School District holds their graduation ceremony at the Potter's House, a nondenominational church, which is used because it can seat more people than any school owned facility. The ACLU threatened to sue the school if it did not change locations.

In Meriden, Connecticut, the city holds the festival of Silver Lights every year which is a large attraction for many people. In 2009, the ACLU complained because Meriden gave the Salvation Army the exclusive right to collect funds at the festival. The ACLU claimed that this showed the city favored a religious institution. The funds, however, only went towards the charity social services.[153]

The big problem that most school districts and school boards have is that they have limited funds with which to fight these kinds of attacks. Typically, rather than fight or defend their position in court, these school boards and school organizations will simply relent to the attacks made by these organizations and individuals threatening law suits. As a result, many of the practices and customs of the country have been dismissed and similar organizations simply follow suit. *Isn't it interesting to see how the country has evolved, since the writing of the Constitution through today, and how the courts have literally swept all religion under the rug?* Remember, the early Supreme Court of the United States unanimously held that a government school should teach Christianity and the Bible, the source of "the purest principles of morality." Modern rulings today are exactly the opposite but few today realize that the earlier courts…courts whose justices were appointed by the Founding Fathers…have already addressed the same issues.

Today, we are so accustomed to hearing the First Amendment coupled with the phrase *"separation of church and state"*, we forget that the word *"separation"*, *"church"*, and *"state"* are not found in any part of the First Amendment. In fact, that phrase appears in no government founding document. Most of us recognize the phrase but few know its source. Yet, it is important to understand the origins of that phrase and its subsequent coupling with the First Amendment. The study of the history of the First Amendment clearly shows that the First Amendment purpose was to limit the Federal Government in two specific areas: (1) the Federal Government was prohibited from establishing a national denomination; (2) the First Amendment barred the Federal Government from interfering with or limiting the people's public religious expressions. This part of the First Amendment is called the Free Exercise Clause *("…or prohibiting the free exercise thereof")*. This Clause required the Federal Government to protect rather than suppress as at present, public religious expression. Because of the Free Exercise Clause, the Federal Government could not prohibit the people's free exercise of religion whether expressed in private or in public.

Note that both religion clauses of the First Amendment were to limit the Federal Government, NOT the people…that is, first, the Government could not establish any national religious denomination and second, the Government could not stop the public religious expressions, but must protect them.

CHAPTER 11

WHEN AMERICA SPURNED GOD

For more than 200 years, America's courts and government followed the teachings and followings of the Founding Fathers and the Constitution. While there have been attempts in early courts to attack the religious beliefs of the Founding Fathers, it wasn't until the early 1960's that America really spurned God. Up to that time, the morality echoed by the United States Government and the Bible were virtually identical. It was that perceived union which inspired the public's reverence for its political system in the first place. Just as it is today, for the most part, Americans in the 1960's were predominately Christian. Displays of the Ten Commandments, the Parables, Gospel quotations and Christian sayings were everywhere. There were prayers in public schools, in public forums, usually all Government affairs and Congress. Public schools conducted Nativity plays. The morality of the society was Judeo-Christian. Forgiveness was an essential principle in the land and factors other than money drove the national mind. Businesses closed their doors on Good Friday. God and Jesus were seen in almost every aspect of American society. Beginning in the 1960's, all that began to erode. All of these were purged from the American scene by Supreme Court rulings.

Perhaps the biggest smack in God's face occurred in 1973, with the U.S. Supreme Court decision of **Roe v. Wade**.[154] This is the Supreme Court decision that created the current abortion law in the United States. In this 1973 decision, the Supreme Court ruled that women had the Constitutional right to an abortion and that this right was based upon an implied right to personal privacy.

In ***Roe v. Wade***, the Supreme Court said that a fetus was not a person, and *"potential life",* does not have constitutional rights of its own. The Court also set up a framework in which a woman's right to an abortion and the state's right to protect potential life shift. Within the first trimester of pregnancy, a woman's privacy right is strongest, and the state may not regulate abortion for any reason. During the second trimester, the state may regulate abortion only to protect the health of the woman. During the third trimester, the state may regulate or prohibit abortion to promote its interest in the potential life of the fetus, except where the abortion is necessary to preserve the woman's life or health.

Basically, the facts in the case were that Roe, the Plaintiff, was a pregnant single woman, who brought a suit challenging the constitutionality of the Texas abortion laws. These laws made it a crime to obtain or attempt an abortion except on medical advice to save the life of the mother. Other plaintiffs in the lawsuit included Hallford, a doctor who faced criminal prosecution for violating the state abortion law, and the Does, a married couple with no children, who sought to stop enforcement of the law on the grounds that it was unconstitutional.

The basic issue was: *do abortion laws that criminalize all abortions, except those required on medical advice to save the life of the mother, violate the Constitution of the United States?*

The Court held YES. State criminal abortion laws except, criminality on a life-saving procedure on the mother's behalf, that do not take into consideration the stage of pregnancy and other interests, are unconstitutional.

What part of "Thou shall not Kill"[155] *does the Court not understand?*

With its decision in Roe the Court undid the abortion regulations of all fifty states. Liberal intellectuals and academic professors helped sell this idea to the public by taking the word *fetus* (Latin for *"very young one"*) to refer to unborn babies defined by the Court's precedents as *"babies whose heads have not cleared the birth canal completely."* As the Fourteenth Amendment was about protecting the civil rights, including the right to life of former slaves, it took the "reasoning" of a Supreme Court justice to turn it around and use it to establish a right to end the lives of unborn children.

It seemed likely to many observers that when the court undertook to decide the case of **Planned Parenthood v Casey**[156], it was going to backtrack on its controversial *Roe* decision Several appointments to the Court by Presidents, who were opposed to *Roe* and who were opposed to judges making laws from the bench *(judicial activism)*, gave the Court an opportunity to reverse *Roe*. Alas, but it was not to be. The Court, not only failed to overturn *Roe*, it also delivered a silly statement of constitutional philosophy where the Court "calls the contending sides of a national controversy to end their national division *(Pro life vs Pro choice)* by accepting a common mandate rooted in the Constitution." Its decision has a special "dimension". The Court claimed to have done this only twice in history: *In Brown v Board of Education*[157] which ended segregation, and *Roe*. *(It is interesting that this Court conveniently overlooked the* **Dred Scott**[158] *decision which settled a "national controversy" by repealing the Missouri Compromise and declaring that blacks could not be citizens, until it was reversed by a Civil War and the Thirteenth, Fourteenth, and Fifteen Amendments to the Constitution! The Thirteenth, Fourteenth and Fifteenth Amendments prohibited slavery and restricted states from enacting any laws that prohibited people of any race, color, or gender from the due process of law.)*

The Court ignored this part of history and said it could not reverse its decision of a controversial case *(Roe)*. "*So to overrule under fire in the absence of the most compelling reason to reexamine a watershed decision would subvert the Court's legitimacy beyond any serious question.*"[159] In the opinion of many legal scholars, the Court has overturned the right of the people of the various states to govern themselves. The Court has also overturned the Tenth Amendment to the Constitution and called it the "rule of law." *(The Tenth Amendment to the Constitution reserves certain powers to the states and not the federal government!)*

Since this initial decision on abortion more than forty years ago, there have been approximately 55 million infants slaughtered. There have been volumes written on the *Roe v. Wade* case arguing both sides of the issue, but that remains the law today. *(And we thought the Holocaust in World War II was bad!)*

The Supreme Cases since *Roe v. Wade* have consistently held the rulings in that case. For example, in **Doe v. Bolton**[160] the Court ruled, a woman's right to an abortion could not be limited by the state, if the abortion was sought for reasons of maternal health. "Mary Doe," who was 9 weeks pregnant, filed suit claiming she was entitled to an abortion under the Constitution because she already had three children and would not be able to support another child. The Court defined health as "all factors---physical, emotional, psychological, familial, and the woman's age---relevant to the well being of the patient." This health exception expanded the right to abortion for any reason through all three trimesters of pregnancy.

Planned Parenthood v. Danforth[161] Here, the Supreme Court invalidated broad portions of Missouri's abortion law including those which banned abortions by saline injection. It required a married woman to obtain the consent of her husband prior to an abortion and required the consent of parents before an abortion could be performed on their minor daughter. The Court concluded that spousal and parental consent requirements amounted to an unconstitutional "veto power" over a decision which should be left to the "medical judgment of the pregnant woman's attending physician", according to *Roe*. The Court struck down the prohibition on saline abortions after 12 weeks, calling it an *"arbitrary regulation designed to prevent the vast majority of abortions"*, and also struck down the duty of care provision, because it required a doctor to preserve the baby's life whatever the stage of pregnancy. *Can you believe that???*

In 1983, in the case of **City of Akron v. Akron Center for Reproductive Health**[162], the Supreme Court threw out the informed consent requirement that included providing information on the medical risk of abortion, fetal development, and alternatives to abortion in a 24 hour waiting period. It also invalidated provisions related to parental consent without judicial review, a provision requiring abortions to be performed only in hospitals after the first trimester and a requirement that fetal remains be disposed of in a "humane and sanitary" manner.

The court ruled unconstitutional, Nebraska's ban on partial birth abortion in the case of **Stenberg v. Carhart**[163]. The Court cited two grounds for striking down Nebraska's law *(and, by implication more than two dozen other similar state laws)*: the absence of an exception to the ban for the "health of the mother" and because the Court found the description of the partial birth abortion procedure to be "vague" and potentially including other mid and late term abortion procedures.

Recent polls indicate that America is split down the center roughly with about 50% against abortions and 50% for abortions. God has to be thoroughly disappointed in America. If one can terminate an infant at 4 weeks, why not at 6 weeks? If, at 8 months, why not at 9 months? If at partial birth, why not just after birth? And, if after birth, why not at any time after that? If it is a dependency issue, babies are just as dependent as an infant in the uterus. Without the mother, they would die. So where does the right to terminate truly end? Do you think for a minute that God, who created life, was responsible for the founding of our country, and who commanded that *"thou shall not kill,"* would be happy with this stand?

If authorizing the killing of infants in abortions was not enough, the Supreme Court established a right to engage in homosexual activity (sodomy)! In light of the long standing tradition, the American people have never amended the Constitution to create a right to homosexual sodomy. But the Supreme Court did that for us! The Court simply decided there should be such a right, and overturned state laws and its own previous ruling *(which it could not do with Roe)! Imagine that!!*

The case of **Romer v Evans (1996)**[164] involved a state constitutional amendment. It was approved by the people of Colorado, which stated: *"Neither the state of Colorado, through any of its branches or departments, nor any of it agencies, political subdivisions, municipalities or school districts, shall enact, adopt or enforce any statute, regulation, ordinance or policy whereby homosexual, lesbian or bisexual orientation, conduct or practices or relationships shall constitute or otherwise be the basis of, or entitle any person or class of persons to have or claim any minority status, quota preferences, protected status or claim of discrimination. This Section of the Constitution shall be in all respects self-executing."* In other words, self-identified homosexuals were denied any special minority privileges and were to be treated like any other Colorado citizen! Sounds fair enough…right?

The Supreme Court, however, overturned the right of the people of Colorado to govern themselves and said that, of course, the Constitution meant that state officials must be left free to provide special privileges for self-identified homosexuals. The Court reasoned that homosexuals could not be denied the opportunity to seek special privileges from state and local officials. The majority of the Court ruled invalid the commonly held position that homosexuality is about conduct, not identity. The Court used its limitless judicial power to disallow state policies with which it disagreed.

Here, as in *Roe*, the Court simply preempted a legislative political debate; as it has in virtually every instance since 1937, it took the side of the leftward-most of the contending forces against the traditional, coincidentally Christian, position.

Predictably, the Court followed its *Romer* thinking in **Lawrence v Texas (2003)**[165] where the Court declared a constitutional right to homosexual sodomy! Here Police found two men engaged in sexual conduct in their home and arrested under a Texas law that prohibited such conduct between two men. The issue was whether a state law prohibiting specific sex acts violated the U.S. Constitution. The Court here held YES, intimate sexual conduct, between consenting adults, is a liberty protected under the Constitution.

The alleged intellectual class, in support of the Court's *Lawrence* "legislation" *(call it "legislation" because is was absolutely not founded on any Constitutional provision or on any traditional conception of the role of judges and the function of a written federal constitution)*, shouted down critics who asked, if private homosexual sodomy was constitutionally protected, why bestiality *(sex with animals)*, incest, and group sex were not! The critics may have shouted down the people who asked that question; BUT, the critics did not answer the question!!!!

Chapter 12

The Last Word

We have seen how America has evicted God from public society across the entire spectrum of the American Governmental system. From the early 60's to this date, not only has prayer been outlawed, God's very name has been declared anti to the United States Constitution, and it has been forbidden to be mentioned in any Federal, state, county, city or municipal context. Not only is prayer forbidden in the public forum, but the display of the cross has been forbidden, the Ten Commandments have been forbidden, the Bible has been forbidden, Nativity plays have been forbidden, even the mere mention of the names *"God"* or *"Jesus"* in schools are now forbidden. Further, anything even suggestive of those names is forbidden.

You ask, where was God when all the public shootings and violence was occurring? Answer: The courts and Congress have thrown God out of the public arena. For all intents and purposes, the Supreme Court has ruled the U.S. Constitution a godless document. The godly does not even have a place in it. The Atheist not only has a place in it, they now own it. The realization of that horrifying thought should leave America aghast.

You have now read about the history of America leaving God and what has caused it. Has it turned around? Is America headed back to the Biblical teachings and God's Word? The answer is NO. Here are some recent events that you may not have read about.

*(1) **Veterans Affairs Houston**:* The Department of Veterans Affairs and its Director of the Houston National Cemetery, Arleen Ocasio, are engaging in religious viewpoint discrimination directly in violation of the first Amendment to the Constitution. Director Ocasio told the Honor Guard that they could not say "May God grant you grace, mercy and peace" to grieving families even if the families request it. Not only that, but the VA forbids mention of God at funerals and requires families to submit prayer for prior approval of the Government; the VA instructs the VFW (Veterans of Foreign Wars) and a private funeral home, that they may not present the option of prayer to families at funerals; the VA tells Volunteers to Remove "God Bless" from Condolence Cards to Grieving families; and the VA closed the Cemetery Chapel and uses it for storage. The Veterans are fighting this attack on free speech and freedoms.

*(2) **Salazar v. Buono**:*[166] The case arose when a former National Park Service (NPS) employee sued for the removal of a seven-foot-tall cross erected in the Mojave Desert in 1934, as a war memorial to honor all fallen soldiers. Following attempts by Congress to designate the cross as a national memorial and to transfer the land to the VFW, the District Court and Ninth Circuit Court both ruled that the cross is unconstitutional and must be removed. The memorial is currently covered with a plywood box, awaiting a ruling by the U.S. Supreme Court. The case, which is part of a larger trend to remove all religious imagery from the public square by groups like the ACLU, could impact thousands of other memorials nationwide. Visit www.donttearmedown.com for more information.

*(3) **Hannah Giles' Legal Defense Fund**:* In the summer of 2009, 20-year-old college student Hannah Giles spent her summer working with James O'Keefe to expose ACORN corruption. Together, they released videos from six cities showing ACORN employees encouraging the duo, posing as a prostitute and pimp, to break laws including tax laws and underage

prostitution. Since the release of the videos, ACORN and two of its former employees filed a $5 million lawsuit against Hannah, James, and Andrew Breitbart, who helped popularize the videos through his BigGovernment.com website. After the suit was dismissed, a third ACORN official, this one in Philadelphia, filed suit. This case is just starting in Federal Court in Philadelphia. Liberty Institute represents Hannah to protect the free speech of citizen journalists and has established www.DefendHannah.com as her legal defense fund.

(4) **Shatkin, et al. v. University of Texas at Arlington**: Two women were fired from their jobs at the University of Texas at Arlington (UTA) because they privately prayed after work for an absent co-worker. After UTA denied all administrative appeals of such termination, the women filed suit against UTA for religious discrimination. The case is currently in litigation.

(5) **Morgan, et al. v. Plano I.S.D.**: A 3rd grade boy was told by school officials that he could not include a religious message in his goodie bags that he was bringing to the "Winter Party" to share with his classmates. The student wanted to include the story of the candy cane, along with candy cane pens, which he and his classmates were encouraged to bring to the school party. However, school officials prohibited anything that was religious from being in the goodie bags, including the story of the candy cane. A lawsuit was filed on behalf of the Morgans, other students, and parents suffering religious discrimination at the hands of the district. A federal judge issued a Temporary Restraining Order against Plano ISD to allow students to bring religious items to the "Winter Party." This ongoing case will impact the freedoms of millions of students nationwide.

(6) **Keep military members out of church**: Retired Vice Admiral Bob Scarborough of Arlington Virginia wrote the following:

"I wanted to give you some disturbing information about the present administration. I work with the Catch-a-Dream Foundation, which provides hunting and fishing trips to children

with life threatening illnesses, many of which are terminal. This past weekend we had our annual banquet/fundraiser event in Starkville. As a part of our program, we had scheduled Sgt. 1st Class Greg Stube, a highly decorated US Army Green Beret and inspirational speaker who was severely injured while deployed overseas and didn't have much of a chance for survival to come. Greg is stationed at Ft. Bragg, North Carolina and received per mission from his commanding officer to come to speak at our function. Everything was on go until the present administration made a policy that NO U.S. SERVICEMAN CAN SPEAK AT ANY FAITH-BASED PUBLIC EVENTS ANYMORE. Needless to say, Greg had to cancel his speaking event with us...Didn't know if anyone was aware of this new policy. Wonder what kind of news we will receive next. Your religion is next on the list. This is just how the Nazis did it in the 30's, slowly one step at a time. If you don't see the similarities you are truly blind."

And sometimes Freedom wins:

> **(7) Lawsuit Against National Day of Prayer Dismissed:**[167] Seventh Circuit Court Says "Hurt Feelings Differ from Legal Injury" Dallas, Texas, April 14, 2011 — Today, the U.S. Court of Appeals for the Seventh Circuit dismissed the Freedom From Religion Foundation's (FFRF) lawsuit attacking the federal government's observance of National Day of Prayer, ruling that the atheists do not have legal standing to bring the suit. *"We applaud the Seventh Circuit's dismissal of this desperate attempt to erase our country's rich history of calling for prayer,"* said Kelly Shackelford, president/CEO for Liberty Institute. *"Sadly, some are determined to censor religious expression in the public arena. As long as Liberty Institute exists and the Constitution is in place, we will do everything in our power to ensure that never happens."*

This ruling, which strongly rejects FFRF's opposition to government's observance of National Day of Prayer, says that being excluded or *"hurt feelings differ from legal injury."*

Despite numerous rulings from the U.S. Supreme Court that protect long-standing traditions of religious invocations, recently, U.S. District Judge Barbara Crabb ruled that the federal government's observation of prayer was unconstitutional. When Congress passed a statute in 1952 calling for the President to issue a proclamation designating the National Day of Prayer, it memorialized the virtually unbroken tradition of Presidents from Washington to Obama who designated a day of prayer.

"The 7th Circuit's decision in **Freedom From Religion Foundation v. Obama** once again affirms what the vast majority of Americans know intuitively: that we should not, and indeed cannot, separate our nation's history from the influence of religion on its founders," said Brad Miller, director of family policy councils for Citizenlink. "Even Americans with a decidedly agnostic view of religion cannot refute the important role religious tradition has played throughout the history of this great nation. The President's proclamation is simply a continuation of a long and deep tradition of urging and acknowledging prayer as a fundamental part of a healthy society. We applaud this decision and the great work of our allies at the Liberty Institute for their work on behalf of religious freedom."

(8) *Plano Vietnamese Baptist Church (PVBC), et al. v. City of Plano*: Despite following all the proper procedures for purchasing the property, the church was denied occupancy because the property did not meet the city's 2-acre site requirement for churches. Members of the congregation had donated their life savings to buy the property only to be told by the city they could not meet there, even though the property originally was built as a church several years ago. In the lawsuit it was demanded that the 2-acre rule be declared an unconstitutional ordinance that discriminates against small churches. The court ruled it to be unconstitutional.

(9) *Croft, et al. v. Governor of Texas.*: A lawsuit was filed against the State of Texas by an atheist who objected to the word "pray" in the Texas Moment of Silence Statute. A group of public school students filed a suit to protect the state's law, which allows a minute of silence for students to pray, meditate or reflect. The statute was upheld in the Federal Court of Appeals.

(10) Templo Bautista Nueva Jerusalen v. City of Duncanville: The City of Duncanville was using zoning laws to discriminate against the church to deny the congregation religious freedom to gather and hold services. After purchasing the building in the downtown area, the church was told a special use permit would be required in order to begin using the building for services. Templo Bautista applied for the permit, and paid the necessary fees but was still denied use of the building because one land owner was opposed to the church being in the neighborhood. A demand letter was sent to the City and a new hearing was granted. Only then did the City agree to allow the church to occupy the building and begin to hold church services.

(11) Pleasant Grove City et al. v. Summum: The American Legion, Veterans of Foreign Wars of the United States, and a number of other national veterans groups filed a brief defending veteran's memorials. The brief sought to overturn the 10th Circuit Court of Appeals ruling which stated cities must allow all privately donated monuments in public areas, regardless of the monument's message or purpose, or not allow any monuments at all. The U.S. Supreme Court ruled in favor of a city's free speech which protect the veterans, and their memorials.

(12) Pastor Rick Barr and Philemon Homes, Inc. v City of Sinton: A pastor and a Christian organization, that provided housing and religious instruction to men after being released from prison for misdemeanor offenses, was banned by the city from existing anywhere in its city limits. It argued at the Texas Supreme Court to reverse the decisions from lower courts. In a landmark decision, the Texas Supreme Court reversed the lower courts and allowed the group in the city! Moreover, this case is historic in that it is the first in Texas history interpreting RFRA (the Texas Religious Freedoms Restoration Act) and is already being used as a model nationwide in protecting religious freedom.

(13) Barrow v. Greenville I.S.D.: Mrs. Barrow, a 15-year teacher with her principal's certificate for 10 years, was told by the Superintendent that she could only have the assistant principal ship for which she was recommended if she agreed to take her own children out of Christian school. When Mrs. Barrow explained her religious objections to removing her children, she was denied the position. Barrow brought suit against the school district to defend the rights of Christian parents to choose religious education for their children without government retribution. The U.S. District Court in Dallas ruled that the right of parents to choose private education was not a fundamental right and thus ruled against Mrs. Barrow. The case was appealed and won a 3 to 0 reversal before the Federal Court of Appeals. Following a two-week jury trial, the jury found that the superintendent had violated Ms. Barrow's constitutional parental rights and awarded Ms. Barrow lost wages and punitive damages and ordered the superintendent to pay her legal fees.

(14) HEB Ministries v. Texas Higher Education Coordinating Board: Tyndale Seminary was fined $173,000 by the state for using the word "seminary" and issuing theological degrees without receiving government approval. The School filed suit in district court against the state for violating the U.S. and state constitutions. The suit, on behalf of Tyndale as well as other seminaries across the state, argued that government attempts to control the religious training of seminaries are unconstitutional. The Austin Court of Appeals ruled in favor of the state and the case was appealed to the Texas Supreme Court. The Texas Supreme Court ruled in favor of Tyndale, in a land mark ruling, stating the law intrudes upon religious freedom protected by the U.S. and Texas Constitutions.

God has been and is being stripped from all aspects of the American government. It has been a national purge. The consequences have been enormous. Out went Christmas, the public decorations and displays, the writing, the moral lessons, the Ten Commandments, the Nativity plays in schools and on and on and on. There have been many subsequent decisions beginning in the 1960's, but the Court has never wavered in its initial assessment. The Courts and Congress have ruled that God has no place in our Constitution and, therefore, no place in our governmental society. They made God the forbidden fruit of the nation. His name could not be mentioned in the public forum, His son's name could not be mentioned, nor could His words or Commandments be seen or discussed especially by the nation's school children. So deadly is the idea of God to our Supreme Court and government that communist leader, Karl Marx, can be mentioned and Marx's words can be taught, but not Christ! A lyric by John Lennon can hang in the courthouse, but not the Ten Commandments.

With heads spinning, the people have tried to comprehend this seemingly illogical interpretation of the Supreme Court concerning the separation of church and state. *How can it be twisted to mean the expulsion of God from the American public arena? How could it be used to shred our former way of life and strip it naked of God? How could it mean the word "God" is now a forbidden term in school or any other governmental institution? How could it come to mean that a historic cross on a county seal had to be removed?*

What are the consequences for throwing God out of America? Will this separation between God and government remove the shield of grace that has guarded our country since its inception? If so, what can we expect? Did God send us any warning, any sign?

Isn't it interesting that just 5 months after the American Supreme Court threw out prayer in the schools, the President of the United States was assassinated? John Kennedy fell to an assassin's bullet in Dallas, Texas. Just months after that, President Johnson plunged the United States into the Viet Nam war. Using the Gulf of Tonkin as an excuse, Johnson ordered 400,000 troops sent to Viet Nam to replace 15,000 American advisers who were there when he was elected President. The war he pushed lasted ten years and killed and maimed or wounded over 200,000 Americans.

What had the Biblical prophecies' warned: assassinations, wars, earthquakes and tidal waves? Exactly 9 months after the Supreme Court ruling removing prayer from public schools, the final signs were delivered on Good Friday, the anniversary of the Lord's crucifixion. On that day in April of 1964, the United States suffered its worst earthquake and tidal wave in recorded history, a 9.2 earthquake. The earthquake shattered Alaska and sent a tidal wave roaring across the Pacific coastline obliterating towns all across Alaska before smashing its way southward affecting cities all the way to the port of Los Angeles, where, even in that distant city, it inflicted millions in damage. And these are only a few of the incidents!

But that is just the warning.

The following American traditions and a major part of our culture are currently under attack by the ACLU, The Freedom from Religion and other anti-religion groups in the country in their Anti-Christian agenda:

- Remove nativity scenes from all public property
- Ban songs such as Silent Night from public schools
- Refuse to allow students to write about the Christian aspect of Christmas in school projects
- Rename Christmas break "Winter" break
- Refuse to allow a city sponsored Christmas Parade to be called a Christmas parade
- Not allow a Christmas tree in a public school
- Rename a Christmas tree displayed on public property a Holiday Tree

In addition to their war on Christians, the ACLU uses their funds to:

- Sue states to force them to legalize homosexual marriages
- Force libraries to remove porn filters from their computers
- Sue the Boy Scouts to force them to accept homosexuals as scout leaders
- Help legalize child pornography
- Legalize sex acts in bars in Oregon
- Censor student led prayer at graduation
- Remove "under God" from the pledge allegiance of the United States
- Remove "In God We Trust" from all our currency.
- Protect the North American Man Boy Love Association whose motto is "sex by eight or its too late!"

Yes, the United States is under attack on a daily basis in all forms of anti-religious attacks by the anti-religious groups through intimidation and law suits. Because of the expense of defending these kinds of suits, most schools, and companies/organizations simply cower down to the demands rather than fight them. They rule money over principles!!! Groups like the Freedom from Religion and the ACLU know that the average group or church cannot bear the legal costs to fight legislation that will remove personal and religious freedoms. Therefore, the group or church will be forced to go along with the changes, or face the consequences.

If you think all the changes to our culture and laws thus far have destroyed the moral fiber of America, don't be surprised if, in the future, the Supreme Court or some lower courts will reach the following conclusions:[168]

- Hate crime laws, with their claim that "hate speech" is verbal violence, will make any criticism of homosexuals or Muslims punishable, even if the remarks are made in a church or synagogue. This includes reading from the Bible or comments related to biblical passages. Crimes against homosexuals will be deemed worth of greater punishment than crimes against others.
- Schools would be legally able to punish any child who does not participate in the celebration of the homosexual lobby and its agenda.
- Reversing a previous decision by the Supreme Court, a new judgment might find that partial birth abortion is protected by the Constitution. So is Euthanasia.
- Parents who oppose their child's decision to have an abortion (even if the child is under 18) are held to be abusive and liable to have their children removed from their home. Abortion is thus seen to be an absolute right.
- Same sex marriage is found in the Constitution and is deemed an inherent right. There can be no discrimination between hetero sexual and homosexual marriages in matters of adoption, the teaching of children in school, and organizations such as the Boy Scouts.

- Churches cannot discriminate against homosexuals in their hiring practices for youth workers, associate pastors, worship leaders, etc. Only the Senior Pastor can be exempt from this requirement because he is primary teacher in the congregation.
- Schools can teach homosexuality beginning in the first grade and parents have no right to withdraw the child from these classes.
- Churches that fail to marry homosexuals will lose their tax-exempt status.
- Homeschooling is found to be unconstitutional unless the curriculum is approved by the state Department of Education and the child is tested by school authorities. The student must be taught about evolution, sexuality, etc.
- The government will implement the "Fairness Doctrine" which says that whenever a controversial issue is presented (e.g. that Jesus is the only way to God, etc.) equal time has to be given to a different point of view in the interest of "Fairness." This, in effect, will put and end to religious radio and talk programs as we know them today.
- Bible studies with more than ten people attending cannot be held in homes without a religious permit that must be furnished by the city/county where the meetings are held.
- Laws could be created that would criminalize all public expressions of religion (especially Christianity). This could include severe penalties for those who would pray at any public event, even if the prayer is voluntary and denominationally neutral. All expressions of religion in schools, businesses, government, and the workplace are strictly forbidden. No Bible or Torah on the desk, no Christian poster or cross will be allowed in the workplace.
- All public crosses are to be removed; no memorial in the shape of a cross is permitted.

Fortunately, these are **NOT THE LAW** yet; but, there are threats and suits involving each of these issues on the horizon. *So, just be aware that they could happen!!!*

We have talked about the Courts and to a lesser extent Congress and state legislatures, what about the Presidents?

Presidents over the years of America have ranged from very Biblically friendly Presidents, George Washington, John Adams, Thomas Jefferson, Jimmy Carter, John Kennedy, Ronald Reagan, to name few, to the most Biblically hostile present President Obama. Here are a few of the more than 55 acts of hostility that President Obama has had toward people of Biblical faith:

April 2009 ---When speaking at Georgetown university, the President ordered a monogram symbolizing Jesus' name be covered when is making his speech.[169]

May 2009---President declines to host services for the National Day of Prayer (a day established by President Eisenhower and enacted into law) at the White House.[170]

May 2009---While President Obama does not host any National Day of Prayer event at the White House, he does host White House Iftar dinners in honor of Ramadan (Muslim event).[171]

October 2010---President Obama begins deliberately omitting the phrase about "The Creator" when quoting the Declaration of Independence---an omission he has made on no less than 7 occasions.[172]

May 12, 2012---The President opposed legislation to protect the rights of conscience for military chaplains who do not wish to perform same-sex marriages in violation of their strongly held religious beliefs.[173]

And the list goes on. Each President has acted on their own belief systems, some religious and other not so much.

President Reagan perhaps gave one of the best descriptions of the beliefs of a sitting President to date in an address to the Bel Aire Presbyterian Church in 1982 when he said:

"Someone asked me whether I was aware of all the people out there who were praying for the President and I had to say, "Yes I am." I felt it and I believe in intercessionary prayer. But I couldn't help but say to that questioner after, sometimes when he was praying, if he got a busy signal, it was just me in there ahead of him. I think I understand how Abraham Lincoln felt when he said, "I have been driven many times to my knees by the overwhelming conviction that I have nowhere else to go."

"Now I realize that it's fashionable in some circles to believe that no one in government should encourage others to read the Bible. We are told that we will violate the Constitutional separation of church and state established by the Founding Fathers in the First Amendment. The First Amendment was not written to protect people and their laws from religious values, it was written to protect those values from government tyranny.

"I've said that we must be cautious and in claiming that God is on our side. I think that the real question we must answer is, "Are we on His side?" No matter where we live, we have a promise that can make all the difference. A promise from Jesus to soothe our sorrows, heal our hearts and drive away our fears. He promised there will never be a dark night that does not end. Our weeping may endure for the night but joy cometh in the morning. He promised if our hearts are true, His love will be as sure as sunlight. And, by dying for us, Jesus showed how far our love should be ready to go. All the way, for God so loved the world that He gave His only begotten Son that whosoever believes in Him should not perish but have everlasting life.

"Americans yearn to explore life's deepest truths and to say their entertainment, or their idea of entertainment is sex and violence and crime is an insult to their goodness and intelligence. We are people who believe love can triumph over hate, creativity over destruction and hope over despair. And that's why so many millions hunger for God's good news.

"I've always believed that we were each of us put here for a reason, that there is a plan, somehow a divine plan for all of us. I know now that whatever days are left to me, belong to Him. I also believe this blessed land was set apart in a very special way. Our forbearers came not for gold but mainly in search of God and the freedom to worship in their own way. We've been a free people living under the law with faith in our maker and in our future.

"I've said before that the most sublime picture in American history is of George Washington on his knees in the snow at Valley Forge. That image personifies a people who know that it is not enough to depend on our own courage and goodness, we must also seek help from God our Father and preserver.

"We'll never find every answer, solve every problem or heal every wound, but we can do a lot if we walk together down that one path that we *know provides real hope. The morality and values such faith implies are deeply embedded in our national character. Our country embraces those principles by design and we abandon them at our peril.*

My experience, in this office I hold, is only deepened by the belief I have held for many years. Within the covers of that single Book are all the answers to all the problems that face us today if we'd only read and believe."[174] Ronald Reagan, President.

History teaches us lessons IF WE WILL ONLY LEARN FROM THEM!

"The experience of Nazi Germany in World War II, reminds us that whoever controls a nation's laws also controls a nation's moral values. It has been observed that behind every system of law there is a god; 'If the source of the law is the individual, then the individual is the god of that system…if the source of law is our court, then the court is our god. If there is no higher law beyond man, then man is his own god… When you choose your authority, you choose your god, and when you look for your law, there is your god.'[175] *Look behind the law and there is your god!"*[176]

It is often asked, *Where was God in the school shootings in Colorado, California, Chicago and in Connecticut? In the disasters with Hurricane Katrina, and Hurricane Sandy?* He was there once, but **America threw Him out!!**

Chapter 13

Enemies Of The First Amendment

So far you have seen the problem with rogue judges and justices, with Congressional actions and the court system. *But what about others who want to remove all religion from our culture?*

Let's look at a few. First, are the two main organizations that routinely attack religion in the courts.

ACLU—American Civil Liberties Union: The ACLU was formed in the early 1920s. Its roots were among socialists and communists who where opposing World War I. Its founder, Roger Baldwin, was a draft dodger who went to prison. Among the early board members were outright communists, including William Foster, who was at one time the general secretary of the Communist Party USA and wrote the book, *"Toward Soviet America."*

In his book, *"Bad Samaritans: The ACLU's Relentless Campaign to Erase Faith from the Public Square"*[193], author Jerome Corsi said, "The initial impulse of the ACLU was to fight for a definition of civil liberties that lined up with atheist, communist ideals. Primary among the objectives was to eliminate God. Communist philosopher Karl Marx's idea was that religion was the 'opiate of the people,' so the idea of God has to be broken down to establish the basis for communism, namely scientific materialism, which clashed with the religious conviction of America's Founding Fathers. The Founders believed our rights were inalienable, granted by God, and chief among those was freedom of religion."

Thus, rather than defending the freedoms enshrined in the Bill of Rights, as many today believe the ACLU does, the group's goal has been, from the beginning, to destroy the very basis for those rights, which, as the Declaration of Independence explains, are "endowed by our Creator."

Since the founding in 1920, the ACLU has not only undermined the First Amendment but for decades, has conducted a war on God as you can see from reading some of the cases referenced in this book. The ACLU founders designed the organizational values to erase all vestiges of American's Judeo-Christian principles. "The ACLU strategy," according to Corsi, "was predicated on a determination to wage its war on God in a stealth (hidden) fashion in which the ACLU intends to destroy religious freedom by appearing on the scene as a defender of religious freedom. For decades the ACLU has beaten and robbed the First Amendment's statement or religious freedom to the point that Judeo-Christian believers have been left lying by the side of the road as if abandoned to die."

The ACLU has done more damage to America's loss of a moral compass than perhaps any other organization outside the judicial system. ***Remember this, if the ACLU wins its war on God, the founding documents of our country… The Declaration of Independence, The Constitution and the Bill of Rights… will not be worth the parchment on which they were written.***

FFRF--Freedom from Religion Foundation: This organization was founded in Wisconsin in 1977. The purposes of the Freedom From Religion Foundation, Inc., as stated in its bylaws, are to promote the constitutional principle of separation of state and church, and to educate the public on matters relating to non-theism (belief in no God--Atheism). FFRF is a member of Atheist Alliance International (AAI). The FFRF has brought more than 40 anti- religion lawsuits since its founding, including, in November 1993, the FFRF successfully went to court to stop the Denver mayor's office from cosponsoring a National Day of Prayer, obtained a court decision that Wisconsin's Good Friday legal holiday is unconstitutional, stopped Bible students at William Jennings Bryan college from giving volunteer religious instruction to students at local schools in Dayton, Tennessee (home of the original Scopes trial on evolution), took the County of Manitowoc, Wis., to court in mid-Dec. 2008 over its "provocative and divisive" prominent display every December since 1946 of a nativity scene bearing the words "Glory to God in the Highest" on its courthouse lawn, joined with the ACLU in a suit *(imagine that!!!)* against the School Board of Giles County, Va., for unconstitutionally endorsing religion by displaying the Ten Commandments on the wall of a district school, filed a lawsuit in federal court to stop faith-based prison programs at the Federal Bureau of Prisons, one of the leading groups in an effort to remove the National Day of Prayer from America's national events each year, and the list goes on. Annie Laurie Gaylor, the Freedom From Religion Foundation (FFRF)'s co-president, insists the Bible has no bearing on the document used to govern the nation. "We have a perfectly Godless and secular Constitution," she said. "There's no Bible, no Jesus, no Holy Scripture in our Constitution." According to the Freedom from Religion Foundation's other co-President Dan Barker, "Christianity is an enemy to humanity, and the antithesis of freedom and religion also poses a danger to mental health, damaging self-respect, personal responsibility, and clarity of thought." The FFRF has recently gone so far as to encourage Catholics to leave the church over the effort by the U.S. Council of Catholic Bishops to gain an exemption for religious-affiliated institutions from the government requirement for coverage for contraception, abortifacients, and sterilization as part of any employee healthcare plan!

In addition, there are many smaller organizations who are active in anti-religious activities. Here are a few:

ARM--ANTI-RELIGIOUS MOVEMENT: "ARM" has become the rather descriptive nick-name for the anti-religion movement, though they don't see themselves as anti-religious at all. They see themselves as lovers of religious freedom and haters only of "destructive cults. There are many fingers to the ARM in the United States -- Citizens Freedom Foundation and Information Service (CFF-IS), American Family Foundation (AFF), Cult Information Center, Spiritual Counterfeits Project, Ex-Moon Inc., Citizens Engaged in Reuniting Families, and more.

MAAF--- Military Association of Atheists & Freethinkers: This is a small group of Atheists who have been active in: removing Bibles from the list of items that are provided in US military approved lodging facilities, forcing the Air Force to remove the word "God" from the logo of its Rapid Capabilities office, forcing the Air Force to remove Bible verses from a military course taught to nuclear missile officers—the ones who push the launch button, forcing the Air Force Academy to drop Operation Christmas Child to provide presents to children at Christmas, and other similar activities against the military. *Why is the Air Force and other military groups bowing down to these kinds of organizations?* "The Air Force has become an easy target for atheists, because they know the Air Force will cave to their anti-religious, anti-Christian demands without a fight," says Tim Wildmon, president of the American Family Association (AFA). "The Air Force has caved to every whim of anti-Christian zealots and the government is content to allow every vestige of religious faith to be silenced."

The Main Stream Media (MSM) (Main newspapers, internet and social media, magazines, television and radio networks!): The former "news" industry has now become an opinion industry. There is very little journalism in the allegedly news industry any more. The industry consists of slanted opinion pieces by talking heads (television and radio), internet and social media blogs and newspaper opinions disguised as "news." Here are a few examples:

Huffington Post: This is an on-line "newspaper formatted website" that frequently has anti-religious slanted articles. As an example, the HP recently promoted the Broadway adaptation of Irish author Colm Toibin's novella *"The Testament of Mary,"* which perverts the biblical Mary of Nazareth into an angry woman bitter over her son Jesus' execution and openly disdainful of His followers. Or, what about the website that recently offered readers a slideshow of the best places to lose one's virginity in San Francisco, and coming in seventh was under the Mount Davidson Cross, one of the city's most beloved religious landmarks.

Washington Post Newspaper: This main stream established old line newspaper that endorses frequent anti-religious events such as aggressively pushing for the gay Left's youth agenda, including a front-page Metro section story on a tiny street protest against the local Boy Scout council: "Among the protesters against the Boy Scouts of America's ban, few have more to risk than a gay Maryland teen," read the headline above a photo. **"Honoring his duty, pursuing equality"** was the large headline.

National Public Radio (NPR): The NPR is a publicly funded national radio network whose "news" and programs are often ant-religious in nature. For example, NPR proved its affinity for publicizing a vicious tale where the Virgin Mary is turned into a bitter atheist who denies the divinity of Jesus and hates the Apostles for trying to spread Christianity among other anti-religious programs. Remember this reason to pledge the next time National Public Radio comes asking for money: "Because we're fond of opportunities to tell American Christians that Jesus isn't God."

TV/Cable networks such as ABC and MSNBC: Religion is a frequent target of "news" and other network programs on America's mainstream television and cable channels. As an example of the programming referenced, ABC wasn't the only network to turn to atheism on Easter morning for some religion-bashing. MSNBC's Melissa Harris-Perry turned to feminist Katha Pollitt to rip apart religions as "all invented by men for men" to repress women.

That came after Harris-Perry somehow compared the morality of abortion as a less weighty matter than access to water in the Third World. Once again, like the week before, Harris-Perry referred to unborn babies as "things," in this case "things in your uterus" that you can evacuate (referring to abortion). Similarly on ABC on Easter morning, George Stephanopoulos invited an atheist on ABC's *This Week* to join a panel discussion about - *wait for it* – religion!

Time Magazine: Not to be outdone in the MSM's attack on Religion, the very liberal Time magazine in its anti-religion slant ran a story that stated, "If your child is religious, he or she may be mentally ill." That's the long and short of the TIME magazine item, *"Can Your Child Be Too Religious?"* published on March 28, 2013, Holy Thursday. Sure, "Religion can be a source of comfort that improves well-being," writer Francine Russo noted, "But some kinds of religiosity could be a sign of deeper mental health issues".

Yahoo News: This relatively new main stream website targeting the same mass audience as Time ran this story: **"Was Mother Teresa actually sort of a jerk?"** The article began, "A new study claims the beloved nun might not have been as helpful to the poor as she could have been."

The anti-religion movies and television shows are way too numerous to mention here and most of you readers recognize them. The point is that America's basic core values and moral compass are constantly being threatened from most all sources from which we receive information!

The common thread in all of these outlets is their anti-religion slant on most "news" articles. Oh sure, they have some pro-religious articles, but these are relatively rare comparatively and are buried deep inside the releases.

It makes one wonder, why do these organizations and their members and writers, detest the very basic Judeo-Christian principles from which America was founded? There is probably no one answer to that question, but rather it depends on the agenda that organization or group is pursuing at the time!

The point here is that the Judeo-Christian principles that have set the moral compass for America since its inception are being, and have been, maligned and attacked from nearly every direction.

Throughout this book I have been talking about "moral compass". *Just what is a moral compass?*

Wiktionary, the on-line dictionary, defines moral compass as: "The full range of virtues, vices, or actions which may affect others and which are available as choices (like the directions on the face of a compass) to a person, to a group, or to people in general." In other words, it's a little voice inside us, like a compass, that tells us the right direction to take when we have to make decisions about right and wrong!

We each develop a moral compass from our education, our environment, our parents, our friends and acquaintances, but more importantly, our study of the Bible or Torah with such values as taught by the Ten Commandments, the Golden Rule, the Beatitudes, and other religious teachings.

Our Founding Fathers reminded us that only a moral people can preserve the liberty *(freedom)* required to build a bright future for America in which individual initiative and free enterprise can thrive once again

Epilogue

Where Do We Go From Here?

From the time America was first founded, we have seen religion stripped away from our culture to the extent that there is no moral compass for the country. Teenage pregnancies are at an all time high, violent crimes are the highest in history, students play with their ipads and smart phones rather than talking to their neighbors or families.

In a country that was founded on Judeo-Christian principles, we seem to be failing at preserving those principles upon which the greatest country in the world was based.

For example, the courts have ruled:

A. It is unconstitutional for the Ten Commandments to be displayed in a solitary setting in public courthouses and government buildings—*despite the fact that the Ten Commandments are a basis of civil law in the Western World and are displayed in many locations throughout the Supreme Court, Capital and other federal buildings.*[177] *(Did you know that there is an aluminum cap at the top of the Washington Monument in Washington with the words "Laus Deo" engraved on the east side? "Laus Deo!" Two seemingly insignificant, unnoticed words…out of sight and, one might think out of mind…but very meaningfully placed at the highest point over what is the most powerful city in the world. And what might those two words (composed of just four syllables and only seven letters) mean? Very simply, they are Latin for,* **"Praise be to God!"** *That means that an expression of worship is the first thing touched every morning by the rays of the Sun on our nation's capital!)*

B. It is unconstitutional for a courtroom to display the Ten Commandments even in a collection of other historic documents related to

American law, such as the Magna Carta, the Declaration of Independence, the Bill of Rights, and the Mayflower Compact.[178]

C. It is unconstitutional for a nativity (Christmas) scene to be displayed on public property unless surrounded by sufficient non-religious displays to prevent it from appearing religious.[179]

D. Even though the actual wording of a legislative bill may be constitutional, the bill becomes unconstitutional if the legislator introducing it had a religious activity in his mind.[180]

E. In Russellville, Kentucky, a library employee was barred from wearing her necklace because it had a small cross on it;[181] and, a school employee in Clymer, Pennsylvania, was suspended for wearing a necklace with a cross.[182]

F. When students are given the latitude of creating artwork of their own choosing, it is unconstitutional for them to include a religious image in their artwork.[183]

G. It is unconstitutional to use a school Public Address system to inform students of a national crisis and ask that they pray for the victims. Furthermore, it is unconstitutional for students to engage in student-led, student-initiated discussions of religion during classroom activities, AND a federally-selected monitor may be appointed in order to ensure compliance with student religious speech prohibitions.[184]

Did you know it was unconstitutional even to see the Ten Commandments at school since students *might voluntarily read, meditate upon, respect, or obey them??*[185]

In Saint Louis, Missouri, when a school official caught an elementary student praying over his lunch; he ordered the student out of his seat, reprimanded him in front of the other students, and took him to the principal who ordered him to stop praying!!![186]

There are hundreds of similar rulings. It is not surprising that an independent poll affirmed that 77 percent of the nation believe the "courts have gone too far in taking religion out of public life" and 59 percent believe that judges have singled out Christianity for attack.[187]

It is interesting to note that, while all of this has occurred since 1947, after the introduction of the "separation" metaphor in the *Everson* case, none of the activities currently restricted or prohibited represent any violation of the actual wording of the First Amendment. The First Amendment places prohibitions against the federal Congress **ONLY** and not on the states, communities, schools, or individuals *(i.e., "Congress shall make no law respecting an establishment of religion or prohibiting the free exercise thereof.")*.

Have the Courts, Congress and the President lost their marbles??

If we continue along the path we have chosen as a nation, I have little doubt that preaching and teaching of any religious beliefs in America will be deemed hate speech. History has proven that the media and propaganda can change a nation!

Remember that in the Introduction I asked the question, *"Suppose you wanted to take over a country and form it like you think it should be, but you wanted to take it over without any military intervention or any shots being fired. How would you do it? Assume that time was not a problem to accomplish this goal. What would you have to change in the country in order to take it over and in what order?"*

The answer was: "The three major things that you would have to destroy are **Patriotism, Morality,** and **Spirituality**." In this book, we have talked about one of these…Spirituality.

The question becomes, WHY do you have to get rid of Spirituality (Religion) to take over a country without a shot being fired? The answer is one of control. If you take away all faith and hope, you are easily subject to the control of others. Remember the old saying, *"If you don't believe in something, you will fall for anything!"* There's your answer. *This has already happened in Germany and Austria in the late 30's!*

So, can it be turned around to regain our moral compass…the glue that holds our culture together?

The answer is YES; however, it is going to take a lot of work and perseverance. I will explain; but, first, let me tell you a story.

When I took the Texas Bar exam to get my law license, there were four essay type questions on the test. Each question was a statement of facts that you, as a lawyer, had to analyze and answer explaining your approach either for or against the facts. On one of the questions, I read and read and read it again but couldn't find anything wrong with the facts. *Pretty strange, e-h-h-h?* I had just had a course in Law School on the Constitution, and the professor had spent the entire quarter discussing "Judicial Activism" which is making new law (legislating) from the bench. So, I wrote my answer based on that class discussion simply because I couldn't find anything else to write about. I just knew I had blown it because I couldn't find anything wrong with one of the questions. Anyway, I took my finished paper to one of the Examiners and turned it in. Before leaving the room, I told the Examiner that since I couldn't find anything wrong with one of the questions, I wrote an essay on Judicial Activism showing how the judge was writing a new law from the bench without the constitutional procedure of going through the Legislature. The Examiner stood up and told me: "Son, there are more than two thousand candidates in this room taking the Bar, and I doubt that there will be more than three of you who catch that!" I suddenly went from scared to death about failing the bar to someone who had just won the lottery!!!

Why am I telling you this story? Because that is one of the problems we have in the country today…***Judicial Activism***…where lifetime appointed federal judges and Supreme Court Justices make new laws from the bench with their decisions! The normal process for a new law is for Congress to pass a bill which, when signed by the President, becomes the law of the land. The courts have become lawmakers and the problems are, they are appointed for life and are not voted into office by the citizens. No matter what Congress or the President does with a law, the court system can declare that law unconstitutional and have it thrown out. *So who is in control of the country? Huh??*

The Supreme Court has been legislating from the bench for the past 50+ years, unlawfully and unconstitutionally stepping outside of their scope of power. This branch has become a treacherous bureaucracy, which grows more corrupt day-by-day, robed in black, and giving the impression that they are a law until themselves, when in fact they aren't.

In 2011, the Supreme Court struck down a California law that would have banned selling "violent" video games to children, stating the games are protected under "free speech." The Court's version of freedom of speech has since created major problems for our culture by allowing children to play current games which teach kids to kill cops, shoot up schools, and to kill other students while being rewarded for their crimes committed. There are video games that teach kids to steal cars, rape women, and even shoot John F. Kennedy dead for a chance to win a $10,000 prize. Then we wonder why America has such a high crime rate!!!

"Liberty is the right to do what the law permits," said Charles Montesquieu. Yet in America today, the present Supreme Court calls it freedom of speech to allow kids to learn how to break the very laws the Court should be enforcing. Crime should be deterred, not encouraged or advocated!!!

Today in America, we need an army of ordinary heroes to stand against the gathering darkness in our country. We need people who will stand for truth courageously, consistently, and with humility and grace. We need to enlist people who know what they believe, why they believe it and how to live out their convictions in all situations.

How do we fix the moral compass (knowing right from wrong)?
This has to be attacked on several fronts:

A. **Judicial**,

B. **Education**, and

C. **Congressional!**

A tall order, but possible.

Here are points that need to be fixed:

* There are only two means of relief from bad judicial decisions: (a) pass a Constitutional Amendment; and/or (b) impeach the judges.

For example, a Constitutional Amendment could put term limits on Supreme Justices and Federal Judges to perhaps 16 years on a rotating basis. No Supreme Court Justice could then serve more than 16 years. *(At the present, there is no limit on how long they may serve!)*

Federal judges are appointed by the President and confirmed by the Senate. So, if a President appoints a liberal or conservative leaning judge, and confirmed by a like minded Senate, you will have the same philosophy in the Court's rulings. That may or may not be good! These appointments are for life! To insure a check and balance in the judicial system, there needs to be some limit on how long a federal judge can be on the bench.

A logical solution to judicial activism is to impeach the rogue judges! Judges who ignore jury decisions, or who pander to politicians while ignoring obvious harm to the society, clearly meet the standards for impeachment set forth in the Federalist Papers *(i.e., "injuries done immediately to society itself"[188])* and also those of the Founding Fathers and early judges, who stated, *"habitual disregard of the public interest should result in impeachment...".*

   * **Judges and Justices must be held accountable!**

Thomas Jefferson warned that: ***"The Constitution...is a mere thing of wax in the hands of the judiciary which they may twist and shape into any form they please."***[189] If impeachment is not soon restored to its original role as a tool to reign in the judges, Jefferson's warning will become reality!

Why is impeachment not pursued get rid of non-elected federal judges?

The answer is that there is no interest on the part of the public to support that action. Several years ago a federal judge threw out a lock tight case based on irrefutable evidence and voluntary confession of drug runners in Florida. Congress was justifiably outraged and called for the judge's removal. The Congress's call for impeachment was attacked vehemently by the media and many judicial leaders around the country. Very few citizens stood up to refute the media's defense of this activist judge by writing letters to the Congressmen, to the editors of newspapers and television, or call in to talk shows, or conducting public demonstrations about the deplorable situation. The public just flat didn't care that a drug running group was set free by a runaway judge! Unless a person has a perception that his dog is in the fight, that person is reluctant to get involved. Judges, who should be impeached and removed from their offices, know this fact and aren't really concerned about losing their jobs.

Every citizen interested in saving this country needs to know the grounds for impeachment and how that process works. **Further, every person must be alert to those judges who abuse or exceed the powers granted to them under the Constitution.** If you hear or read of such a judge, call the newspaper, radio or TV station News Room, or post information on the judge on line or one of the social networks.

   * **Once you learn of the situation, begin by creating a public ground swell on the issue and put pressure on your members of Congress to take steps to impeach the wayward judge.** You can do this by talk-

ing to others, writing letters-to-the-editor, calling talk shows and tweeting others about it with your smart phone. The social media and internet with today's technology is where the control lies with the public. Newspapers, printed magazines, and over the air radio/TV are on the way out and the social media, internet and electronic publications are here already! Congress responds to mandates from people often before the members are willing "to be taken to the woodshed" with public criticism!

* Work to establish a legislative VETO over court decisions by a two-thirds supermajority vote of both houses of Congress. Federal judges and justices must be held accountable for their actions and this is the way to do just that!

* Every member of Congress should be required to read the entire Constitution of the United States and even take a short test on it to show that they have read it!

John Jay the first Supreme Court Chief Justice and a Founder of the Constitution once said:

"Every member of the State ought to diligently read and study the Constitution of his country…By knowing their rights, they will sooner perceive when they are violated and be the better prepared to defend and assert them."[190]

I would guess that about 90% (or even higher) of the members of Congress have never read the entire Constitution WHICH THEY SWEAR TO UPHOLD!! Yet, these are the same people who pass laws reflecting the Constitution. Although the entire Constitution can be read in less than two hours by the average person, less than 1% of the population has even looked at it.

*Every student in the sixth grade and again as a senior in High School should be required to read and study the Constitution and be tested on it to prove they understand it. The Sixth graders learn a little American History which most will forget. They need to be reminded of it before they graduate and enter their adulthood career march and assume the responsibilities of citizenship.

* Every citizen should take an on line course (free) on the Constitution from Hillsdale College by going to <u>https://online.hillsdale.edu/register</u>. You will be amazed at what you don't know and will learn from some of the country's best instructors and teachers. Also, I highly recommend that you subscribe to *Imprimis*, a free monthly publication from the college, that gives you outstanding talks and perspectives from the best Constitutional experts in the country.

    * **Educate the members of Congress on the wayward judges with emails, twitter messages, and phone calls to urge them to begin impeachment proceedings against the most prominent activist judges.** This will attract the attention of the others and act as a deterrent for their acts so they become more restrained in their orders and decisions. Congress acts normally in two ways: (1) by money donations for their reelection efforts and (2) by a ground swell of criticism from their constituents. What do the Chinese say, *"No tickie no washie!!!"* Since America is moving away from being a limited Republic and more towards Socialism/Fascism, and the Chinese are moving more toward democracy, maybe we ought to listen to them, after all, they have been around for several thousand years, and us, just barely 250!

    * **Parents, look at your children's school books and see what they are being taught in school.** You may be very surprised. For example, teachers in North Carolina schools were told what values they should instill in their children. The seven point list:
- There is no right or wrong, only conditioned responses.
- The collective good is more important than the individual.
- Consensus is more important than principle.
- Flexibility is more important than accomplishment.
- Nothing is permanent, except change.
- All ethics are situational; there are no moral absolutes.
- There are no perpetrators, only victims.[191]

Not all public schools subscribe to these agendas but parents must investigate what your children are being taught. If you don't get involved with your children's education, the children will be totally confiscated by a non-spiritual point of view that is foreign to the value system with which most of us were raised. I can only plead with you as a parent or grandparent to take charge of our future, and your children and grandchildren's education. They are America's most precious possession. If you are ever going to be courageous, it has to be NOW. These attacks are eroding our culture and value systems.

* Eliminate tenure for public teachers and college professors. Make them accountable for the quality of instruction they provide students. Tenure has a tendency to create laziness and lower standards in teaching. Especially at a time in America's history, we need all the help it can get in education!

* Require that the school systems and textbook writers create a curricula with textbooks that reinforces actual education and the preservation of the civil society thought core principles and values. Remove such things as multiculturalism and political correctness from the curriculums of education.

* Demand that all public servants, elected or appointed, at all times uphold the Constitution and justify their public acts under the Constitution and the freedoms (liberties) it grants. You would think this would be the case all the time, but guess what, it isn't! Remember, politicians normally react to only two things, money and constituent pressure!

* Know your Religious Rights. The Founding Fathers considered religious liberty our "first freedom" and the glue which holds our country together. All other freedoms in the Constitution are based on this religious liberty. The Founding Fathers understood that our right to worship God, and follow His teachings according to the principles of his religious faith, was the foundation of our society. *"A man whose religious faith was repressed could never be a loyal citizen since the state was usurping his first allegiance and costing him his primary freedom. This is one of the most important distinctions that made America an exceptional nation…if not the most important!"*[192]

The Founding Fathers are probably turning over in their graves today as their America is unrecognizable. The freedom of religion is fighting an uphill battle from well funded and aggressive organizations and individuals, who are using the courts, Congress, the federal bureaucracy, and the media to limit religious freedom. We have seen how this radicalized minority, driven by an anti-religious movement, is turning the First Amendment upside down.

* Government employees should not participate in holidays. Since we can't pray to God, can't Trust in God and cannot post His Commandments in Government buildings, I don't believe Government employees (Federal, State, and Local) should participate in Easter, Christmas, Thanksgiving celebrations which honor God that our government is eliminating from many parts of our lives and culture. That means the Supreme Court should be in session on Christmas, Good Friday, Thanksgiving and Easter as well as Sundays, after all, "it is just another day according to the Congress, White House and courts" The Congress should not have a Christmas break, since "it is just another day!!!" Perhaps a lot of taxpayer money could be saved if all government office and services would work on holidays and Sundays (initially set aside for worshipping God) because, after all, our government and court says that it should "just be another day!!!!" It shouldn't cost any overtime since those would be just like any other day of the week to a government that is trying to be "politically correct."

What do you think? Maybe our elected officials will stop giving in to the "minority opinions" and begin, once again, to represent the "majority" of the American people....The folks that elected them!

What should you do if you are threatened by an anti-religious group? If you, your schools or neighborhoods are threatened or even sued by the anti-religious movement in the country today, you have to fight back or risk losing your liberties (Freedoms). *If I were in that position, the first place I would call for help would be the Liberty Institute in Texas. Their team of attorneys and researchers have never lost a case to the ACLU or Freedom From Religion organization. I have found their aggressive approach to those attacking the First Amendment to be right on target. Check them out at www.libertyinstitute.org on line.*

America is at a serious cross roads and needs help from all of us. Remember the first words to the Constitution of the United States: **"WE the PEOPLE of the United States..."** It was our forefathers who made this country great. It is **WE the People** who are charged with keeping it great if we intend for it to regain its status as a leader of all nations of the world. Speaking through Joshua, God said said, *"Have I not commanded you? Be*

Strong and courageous. Do not be afraid; do not be discouraged, for the Lord your God will be with you wherever you go." Joshua 1:9

GOD DIDN'T LEAVE AMERICA, AMERICA LEFT GOD!

APPENDIX

<u>BIBLE VERSES QUOTED:</u>

ISAIAH 33:22 (NIV) "For the Lord is our judge, The Lord is our lawgiver, the Lord is our king, it is he who will save us."

JEREMIAH 18:9 (NIV) "And if at another time I announce a nation or kingdom is to be built up and planted, and if it does evil in my sight and does not obey me, then I will reconsider the good I had intended to do for it."

DEUTERONOMY 17:6 (NIV) "On the evidence of two witnesses or of three witnesses he that it to die shall be put to death; a person shall not be put to death on the evidence of one witness."

DEUTERONOMY 17:15 (NIV) "…be sure to appoint over you the king the Lord your God chooses. He must be from among your own brothers. Do not place a foreigner over you, one who is not a brother…"

EZEKIEL 18:20 (NIV) "But if the wicked will turn from all his sins that he has committed and keeps my decrees and does what is just and right, he will surely live; he will not die."

EXODUS 18:21 (NIV) "But select capable men from all the people---men who fear God, trustworthy men who hate dishonest gain---and appoint them as officials over thousands, hundreds, fifties and tens."

EZRA 7:24 (NIV) "You are to know that you have no authority to impose taxes, tribute or duty on any of the priests, Levites, singers, gatekeepers, temple servants, or other workers at this house of God."

JOHN 17:3 (NIV) "Now this is eternal life; that they may know you, the only true God, and Jesus Christ, whom you have sent."

AMENDMENTS TO CONSTITUTION REFERENCED:

AMENDMENT # 1
(Ratified December 15, 1791)

Congress shall make no law respecting an establishment of religion, or prohibiting the free exercise thereof; or abridging the freedom of speech, or of the press; or the right of the people peaceably to assemble, and to petition the Government for a redress of grievances.

AMENDMENT #10
(Ratified December 15, 1791)

The Powers not delegated to the United States by the Constitution, nor prohibited by it to the States, are reserved to the States respectively, or to the people.

AMENDMENT #14
(Ratified July 9, 1868)

Section 1. All persons born or naturalized in the United States and subject to the jurisdiction thereof, are citizens of the United States and of the State wherein they reside. No Stated shall make or enforce any law which shall abridge the privileges or immunities of citizens of the United States; nor shall any state deprive any person of like, liberty, or property, without due process of law, nor deny to any person within its jurisdiction the equal protection of the laws.

Section 2. Representatives shall be apportioned among the several States according to their respective numbers, counting the whole number of persons in each State, excluding Indians not taxed. But when the right to vote at any election for the choice of electors for the President and Vice President of the United States, Representatives in Congress, the Executive or Judicial officers of a State or the members of the Legislature thereof, is denied to any of the make inhabitants of such State, being twenty-one years of age, and citizens of the United States, or in any way abridged, except for participation in rebellion, or other crime, the basis of representation therein shall be reduced in the proportion which the number of such make citizens shall bear to the whole number of male citizens twenty-one years of age in such State.

Section 3. No person shall be a Senator or Representative in Congress, or elector of President and Vice President, or hold any office, civil or military, under the United States, or under any State, who, having previously taken an oath, as a member of Congress, or as an officer of the United States, or as a member or judicial officer of any State, to support the Constitution of the Unite States, shall have engaged in insurrection or rebellion against the same, or given aid or comfort to the enemies thereof. But Congress may by a vote of two-thirds of each House, rmove such disability.

Section 4. The validity of the public debt of the United States, authorized by laws, including debts incurred for payment of pensions and bounties for services in suppressing insurrection or rebellion, shall not be questioned. But neither the United Sates nor any State shall assume or pay any debt or obligation incurred in aid of insurrection or rebellion against the United States, or any claim for the loss or emancipation of any slave; but all such debts, obligations and claims shall be held illegal and void.

Section 5. The Congress shall have power to enforce, by appropriate legislation, the provisions of this article.

BIBLIOGRAPHY

(1) Saul Alinsky, *Rules for Radicals*, Random House, NY, (1971)

(2) David Barton, *America's Godly Heritage*, Wall Builders, Box 397, Aledo, TX 76008 (1993)

(3) David Barton, *Four Centuries of American Education*, Wall Builders, Box 397, Aledo, TX 76008 (2004)

(4) David Barton, *Original Intent*, Wall Builders, Box 397, Aledo, TX 76008 (2008)

(5) David Barton, *Restraining Judicial Activism*, Wall Builders, Box 397, Aledo, TX 76008 (2003)

(6) David Barton, *School Prayer and other Religious Speech*, Wall Builders, Box 397, Aledo, TX 76008 (2001)

(7) David Barton, *The Spirit of the American Revolution*, Wall Builders, Box 397, Aledo, TX 76008 (2000)

(8) All Bible references are from the New International Version (NIV).

(9) Jerome Corsi, *Bad Samaritans: The ACLU's Relentless Campaign to Erase Faith from the Public Square*, Thomas Nelson Inc., Nashville, TN (2013)

(10) Kevin R. C. Gutzman, *The Politically Incorrect Guide to the Constitution*, Regnery Publishing, Inc, One Massachusetts Ave, N.W. Washington,. D.C. 20001 (2007)

(11) Kermit Hall, James W. Ely, Joel B. Grossman, *The Oxford Companion to the Supremem Court of the United States*, Oxford University Press (2005)

(12) Mark Levin, *Liberty and Tyranny*, Simon & Schuster, Inc, 1230 Avenue of the Americas, New York NY, 10020, (2009)

(13) Erwin W. Lutzer, *When A Nation Forgets God*, Moody Publishers, 820 N. LaSalle Blvd, Chicago, IL 60610 (2010)

(14) Marlin Maddoux, *Public Education Against America*, (New Kensington, Pa: Whitaker House (2006)

(15) Robert J. McKeever, *The United States Supreme Court: A Political and Legal Analysis*, Manchester University Press (1997)   .

(16) Kelly Shackelford, *Know your Religious Rights*, Liberty Institute, 2001 West Plano Parkway, Suite 1600, Plano TX 75075 (2012)

(17) W. Cleon Skousen, *Cleansing of America*, Ensign Publishing, Box 298, Riverton, UT, 84065 (2010)

(18) W. Cleon Skousen, *The 5000 Year Leap*, National Center for Constitutional Studies, www.nccs.net (2010)

(19) W. Cleon Skousen, *The Naked Communist*, The Reviewer, 2197 Berkley Street, Salt Lake City, UT 84109 (1962)

(20) Robert White, *Awake America*, Creation House, 600 Rinehart Road, Lake Mary, FL 32746 (2008)

END NOTES

IINTRODUCTION
1. Cooper v Aaron (1958), 358 US 1
2. W. Cleon Skousen, The Naked Communist, The Reviewer Publications, Salt Lake City, UT (1971)

CHAPTER 1
3. Benjamin Franklin, The Works of Benjamin Franklin, Jarad Sparks, editor (Boston: Tappan, Whittemore and Mason, (1840), Vol. X, p. 297, to Messrs. The Abbes Chalut and Arnaud, April 17, 1787.
4. John R. Howe, Jr., The Changing Political Thought of John Adams, (N.J.: Princeton University Press, 1966),p.189
5. William V. Wells, The Life and Public Service of Samuel Adams, Boston: Little Brown and Company (1865), 3 Volume set, Vol. 1, p22, essay published in The Public Advertiser, 1748
6. David Barton, God in the Constitution, Wallbuilders, Aledo Texas (2013)
7. James Madison, Federalist Papers, No. 14, p. 100
8. Benjamin Pierce, A History of Harvard University (Cambridge, MA: Brown Shattuck and Co., 1833, Appendix, p. 5.
9. Ibid
10. The catalogue of the library of Yale College in New Haven (New London; T. Green, 1743 prefatory remarks).
11. The Laws of the Old College in New Haven, Connecticut (New Haven: Josiah Meigs, 1787), pp. 5-6, Chapter II, Article I, 4.
12. The Laws of the College of New Jersey (Trenton: Isaac Collins, 1794), p. 5.
13. Thomas Jefferson Wertenbaker, Princeton: 1746-1896 (Princeton: Princeton university Press, 1946) p 88. Lawrence A Cremin, American

Education: The Colonial Experience, 1607-1784 (New York, Evanston, and London: Harper & Row, 1970) p. 301; Nation Under God: A Religious Patriotic Anthology, Frances Brentano, editor(Great Neck, NY: Channel Press, 1957) pp. 41042; Dr. John Eidsmoe, Christianity and the Constitution (Grand Rapids: Baker Books, 1987) p.83; Alexander, Princeton College During the Eighteenth Century, pp. 121-185.

14. Elias Boudinot, An Oration Delivered at Elizabeth-Town, New Jersey, Agreeably to a Resolution of the States of Society of Cincinnati on the Fourth of July, 1793 (Elizabeth-Town:

15. Bernard Steiner, The Life and Correspondence of James McHenry (Cleveland: The Burrow Brothers, 1907) p. 475; in a letter from Charles Carroll to James McHenry of November 4, 1800.

16. See The Papers of Benjamin Franklin, Vol.7, pp 100-101; letter from John Waring to Benjamin Franklin on January 24, 1757; p. 356, letter from Benjamin Franklin to John Waring on January 3, 1758.

17. See Benjamin Rush's January 14, 1795 letter to Pennsylvania Abolition Society, Benjamin Rush, Letters of Benjamin Rush, L.H. Butterfield, editor (Princeton University Press, 1951) Vol. II, pp. 757-758.

18. Benjamin Rush, Essays, Literary, Moral and Philosophical (Philadelphia: Thomas and Samuel F. Bradford, 1798), pp. 75-92, "Thoughts upon Female Education, Accommodated to the Present State of Society, Manners, and Government, in the United States of America. Addressed to the Visitors of the Young Ladies Academy in Philadelphia, 28th July 1787."

19. M.E. Bradford, A Worthy Company (Marlborough, NH, Plymouth Rock Foundation, 1982), pp. v-vi.

20. John Sergeant, Eulogy on Charles Carroll of Carrolltown delivered at request of the select and common councils of the city of Philadelphia, December 31, 1832 (Philadelphia; Lydia R. Bailey, 1833), p. 18.

21. The Holy Bible as printed by Robert Aitken and approved and recommended by the Congress of the United States of America in 1782 (Philadelphia: R. Aitken, 1782).

22. John Adams, Works, Vol. X, pp. 45-46, to Thomas Jefferson, June 28, 1813.

23. William Jay, The Life of John Jay (New York: Jay and Jay Harper, 1833, Vol. II, p.376.

24. Church of the Holy Trinity v. United States, 143 US 457, 465,471 (1892).

25. Ibid.

CHAPTER 2
26. The Nuremberg Project, "July 6, 1943—The Nazi Master Plan: The Persecution of the Christian Churches" (at http://www.camlaw.rutgers.edu/publications/law-religion/nuremberg/nurinst1.htm); see also Christianity Today, "Christian History Corner Final Solution Part II" at http://www.christianitytoday.com/et/2002/102/52.0.html).
27. Holocaust Encyclopedia, "The Holocaust" (at www.ushmm.org/wlc/en/index.php?lang=en&ModuleId-10005143) and R. J. Rummel, Death By Government (Transaction Publishers, 1994) p.8.
28. The Works of Benjamin Franklin, Jared Sparks, editor (Tappan, Whittemore and Mason, 1840) Vol. X, p. 282 to Thomas Paine.
29. Democracy in America, translated by George Lawrence, edited by J.P. Mayer (Doubleday & Company 1969)pp 45, 302, 590.
30. Columbia History of Education in Kansas, Compiled by Kansas Educators (Edwin H. Snow, 1893), p. 81.
31. Columbia History of Education in Kansas, p.81
32. Vidal v Girard's Executors, 43 US 126 (1844)
33. Ibid pp. 143 and 152
34. Ibid
35. (Fisher Ames, Notices of the Life and Character of Fisher Ames (T.B. Wait & Co. 1809), pp.134-135.
36. Zorach v Clauson, 343 US 306, 313-314 (1952)
37. David Barton, America: To Pray or not to Pray? (Wallbuilder Press,Aledo, TX, 1994—pp.59-61)
38. www.NationMaster.com, "Education:Literacy Total Population"; See also Texas Litrary Council Developing Human Capital, p.2, (1991)
39. David Barton, Four Centuries of American Education", (Wallbuilder Press Aledo, TX, 2004,p.51)

CHAPTER 3
40. The Holy Trinity Church V United States , 143 US 457, 465, 471 (1892)
41. Ibid

CHAPTER 4

42. Witherspoon, Works, Vol. IV, p95 Sermon XIX, "Seasonable Advice to Young Persons," Feb.12, 1762.
43. Everson v. Board of Education of Ewing Township, 330 U.S. 1 (1947).
44. People of State of Illinois, ex. rel. McCollum v. Board of Education of School District #71, Champagne County, Illinois, 333 U.S. 203 (1948).
45. Id. at p. 212.
46. Zorach v. Clauson, 343 U.S. 306 (1952).
47. Id. at 312-313.
48. Zorach at p. 315.
49. Engle v. Vitale, 370 U.S. 421 (1962).
50. Charles Evans Hughes, the autobiography notes of Charles Evans Hughes, David J. Danelski and Joseph S. Tulchin, eds. (Cambridge, MA: Harvard University Press, 1973, p.44).
51. Trop v. Dulles, 356 U.S. 86, 101 (1958).
52. Abington v. Schempp, 374 U.S. 203, 220-221 (1963).
53. Walsh v. Tax Commissioner of New York City, 397 U.S. 664 (1970)

CHAPTER 5

54. Engle vs. Vitale, 370 US 421 (1962)
55. Id. at p. 434.
56. Id. at p. 435.
57. Engle at p. 445.
58. School District of Abington TP., PA. v. Schempp, 374 U.S. 203 (1963)
59. Id. at p. 225
60. Schempp p.401
61. Joseph Story, Life and Letters of Joseph Story, William W. Story, ed. (Boston: Charles C. Little and James Brown, 1851), Vol. 2, p. 8.
62. William Wirt, Sketches of the Life and Character of Patrick Henry (Philadelphia: James Webster, 1818), p. 402.
63. John Jay; Winning of Peace. Unpublished papers 1780-1784, Richard B. Morris, ed. (New York: Harper and Roe Publishers, 1980), Vol. 2, p. 707, etc.
64. Abingdon v. Schempp, 374 U.S. 203, 217 (1963).
65. Wallace v. Jaffree, 472 U.S. 38 (1985)
66. Constitution (1813), p. 364 "an ordinance of the territory of the United States Northwest of the River Ohio," Article iii.

67. Speeches of the ...Governors...of New York, p. 66, John Jay, November 4, 1800.
68. The papers of Henry Laurens, George C. Rogers, Jr., ed. (Columbia University of South Carolina Press, 1980), Vol. XI, p. 200.
69. Wallace, pp. 113-114 (Rehnquist, J., dissenting).
70. McComb v. Crehan, 320 Fed. Appx. 507.
71. Mellen v. Bunting, 327 F. 3d, p. 355.
72. ACLU of New Jersey v. Blackhorse Pike Regional Board of Education, 84 F. 3d 1471.
73. Workman v. Greenwood Community School Corp., #1:10-0293, 2010 U.S. District Lexis 42813(S.D. Ind. April 30, 2010).
74. Griffith v. Butte School district #1, 244 p. 3d, p. 321 (Mont. 2010).

CHAPTER 6
75. Bible, Exodus chapter 20 verses 3-17
76. Stone v. Graham, 449 U.S. 39 (1980).
77. Stone, p. 41.
78. Id. p. 45.
79. Id. p.46.
80. Lynch v. Donnelly, 465 U.S. 668, 677(1984).
81. Stone, p.42.
82. Witherspoon, Works (1815), Vol. 4, p. 95.
83. Noah Webster, Collection of Papers, pp.291-292. Reply to letter of David McClure on the subject of proper course of study in the Gerrard College, Philadelphia, October 25, 1836.
84. Noah Webster, History, p. 339.

CHAPTER 7
85. Locke v. Davey, 540 U.S. 712 (2004).
86. Lee v. York County School District, 484 F.3d 687 (Fourth Circuit 2007).
87. Peloza v. Capistrano Unified School District, 37 F.3d 517 (Ninth Circuit, 1994).
88. Eulitt,v The Maine Department of Education, 307 F.Supp. 2d 158 (D. Me. Mar. 9, 2004).
89. LaRue v. The Colorado Board of Education, #11-4424 (Colorado District Court, August 12, 2011).

90. Tinker v Des Moines Independent City School District, 393 US 503 (1969)
91. Sante Fe Indep. Sch. Dist. V Doe, 530 US 290, 302 (2000)
92. Guidance on Constitutionally Protected Prayer in Public Elementary and Secondary Schools, U. S. Department of Education, found at www2.ed.gov/policy/gen/guid/religionandschools/prayer_guidance.html.
93. Edwards v. Aguillard, 482 U.S. 578 (1987).
94. Lopez v. Candaele, 630 F.3d 775 (Ninth Circuit 2010).
95. Busch v. Marple Newtown School District, 567 F.3d 89 (Third Circuit 2009).
96. Nurrev v. Whitehead, 580 F.3rd 1087 (Ninth Circuit, 2009).
97. Corder v. Louis Palmer School District #38, 566 F3d 1219 (Tenth Circuit, 2009).
98. Fleming v. Jefferson County School District R-1, 298 F3d 918 (Tenth Circuit, 2002).
99. Furley v Aledo Independent School District, 218 F3d 743 (Fifth Circuit 2000).
100. Settle v. Dickinson County School Board, 53 F3d 152 (Sixth Circuit 1995).
101. Denooyer v. Merinelli, #92-2080, 1993 U.S. Appeals LEXIS 20606 (Sixth Circuit 1993).
102. Eder v City of New York, 2009 U.S. District LEXIS 11501 (S.D. N.Y. February 12, 2009).
103. Kiesinger v. Mexico Academy and Central School, 427 F2d 182 (N.D.N.Y. March 31, 2006).
104. Washegesic v. Bloomingdale Public Schools, 33 F3d 679 (Sixth Circuit 1994).
105. Duran v. Nitsche, 780 Fed Supp 1048 (E.D. PA. 1991).
106. DeSpain v. DeKalb County School District, 384 F2d 836 (Seventh Circuit 1967).
107. Stone v. Graham, 449 U.S. 39, 42 (1980).
108. Washington, Address…prefatory to his declination, pp. 22-23.
109. Debates and proceedings in the Congress of the United States (Washington, D.C.: Gales and Seaton, 1834) Vol. 1, p. 28, by President George Washington, April 30, 1789.
110. Thomas Jefferson, Notes on the State of Virginia (Philadelphia: Matthew Carey, 1794), Query XVIII, p. 237.

CHAPTER 8

111. John Doe 3 v. Elmbrook School District, #10-2922 (Seventh Circuit 2012).
112. Adams v. Trustees of University of North Carolina-Wilmington, 640 F.3rd 550 (Fourth Circuit 2011).
113. Borden v. School District of the Township of East Brunswick, 523 F.3rd 153 (Third Circuit 2008)
114. http://www.Iowastatedaily.com/news/artricle_70ce5c96-4096-11e1-ac1d-0019bb2963f4.html.
115. Roarke v. South Iron R-1 School District, 573 F.3rd 556 (Eighth Circuit 2009).
116. Christian Legal Society Chapter at Arizona State University College of Law, the Crow, #cv04-2572, 2006 U.S. Dist. LEXIS 25579 (D. Arizona 2006).
117. Harrison v. Gregoire, #02-2-01831-3 (Super.Ct. Washington 2002).

CHAPTER 9

118. Hein v. Freedom From Religion Foundation, 551 U.S. 587.
119. Mitchell v. Helms, 530 U.S. 793.
120. Opulent Life Church v. City of Holly Springs, MS, #12-60052 (Fifth Circuit 2012)
121. Centro Familiar Christiano Buenas Neuvas Christian Church v. City of Yuma, 651 F.3d 1163(Ninth Circuit 2011).
122. Glassman v. Arlington County, VA, 628 F.3d 140 (Fourth Circuit 2010).
123. Koniko v. Orange County, 276 Fed. Appx. 916 (Eleventh Circuit 2008).
124. Petra Presbyterian Church v. Village of North Brook, 489 F. 3d 846 (Seventh Circuit 2007).
125. Grace United Methodist Church v. City of Cheyenne, 451 F.3d 643 (Tenth Circuit 2006).
126. Amandola v. Town of Babylon, 251 F.3d 339 (Second Circuit 2001).
127. Calvary Christian Center v. City of Fredericksburg, VA, 832 Fed. Supp. 2d 635 (E.D. VA. November 21, 2011).
128. Family Life Church v. City of Elgin, 561 Fed. Supp. 2d 978 (N.D. Illinois June 18, 2008).
129. Barr v. City of Sinton, 295 S.W. 3d 287 (Tex. 2009).

130. Cambodian Buddhist Society of Connecticut, Inc. v. Planning and Zoning Commission of the Town of Newtown, 941 A.2d 868 (Connecticut 2008).
131. Waltz v. Tax Commission of City of New York, 397 U.S. 664 (1970).
132. Ibid, p.672.
133. Waltz at 716, (Douglas, J., dissenting).
134. Rush, essays, p. 8, "On the mode of education proper in a republic."
135. K. Alan Snyder, Defining Noah Webster: Mind and Morals in the Early Republic (New York: University Press of America, 1990), p. 253, to James Madison, October 16, 1829.
136. An American Dictionary of the English Language (1849), S.V. "Religion".
137. See United States v. Seeger, 380 U.S. 163 (1965) and Welsh v. United States, 398 U.S. 333 (1970).
138. Allegheny v. ACLU, 492 U.S. 573, 590 (1989).
139. See, ACLU v. City of Plattsmouth, 358 F.3d 1020, 1041 (Eighth Circuit 2004; Allegany v. ACLU, 492 U.S. 573, 590 (1989). See also, Internal Revenue Service, "Search for Charities" (at http://www.irs.gov/charities/aricle/0..id=96136.00.html); Newsweek, August 21, 1989, p. 4.
140. Torcaso v. Watkins, 367 U.S. 488, 495 (1961)
141. Church of Scientology Flag Service Organization, Inc. v. City of Clearwater, 2 F3d 1514, 1520 (Eleventh Circuit 1993).
142. Church of Scientology, "Introduction to Scientology (at http://www.Scientology,org/en_US/religion/index.html).
143. Newdow v. U.S. Congress, 292 F3d 597 (Ninth Circuit 2002)

CHAPTER 10
144. Widmar v. Vincent ,454 U.S. 263 (1981)
145. Board of Education of the West Side Community Schools v. Mergens, 496 U.S. 226 (1990)
146. Lambs Chapel v. Center of Moriches Union Free School District, 508 U.S. 384 (1993)
147. Church of the Lukumi Babalu Aye, Inc. v. City of Hialeah, 508 U.S. 520 (1993)
148. Rosenberger v. Rector and Visitors of the University of Virginia, 515 U.S. 819 (1995).
149. Good News Club v. Milford Central School, 533 U.S. 98 (2001).

150. Community House, Inc. v. City of Boise, 490 F3d 1041 (Ninth Circuit 2007).
151. Church on the Rock v. City of Albuquerque, 84 F3d 1273 (Tenth Circuit 1996).
152. http://www.gazette.com/articles/religious/127840-academy-Christmas.html.
153. http://www.religionclause.blogspot.com/2009/12/group-complains-about-cities-favoritism.html

CHAPTER 11
154. Roe v. Wade, 410 U.S. 113 (1973)
155. Thou Shall not Kill, Ten Commandments, Bible at Exodus 20:13.
156. Planned Parenthood v Casey, 505 US 833 (1992)
157. Brown v Board of Education, 347 US 483, (1954)
158. Dred Scott v Standford, 60 US 393 (1857)
159. Roe v Wade, ibid
160. Doe v. Bolton, 410 U.S 179 (1973).
161. Planned Parenthood v. Danforth, 428 U.S. 52 (1976).
162. City of Akron v. Akron Center for Reproductive Health, 462 U.S 416 (1983).
163. Stenberg v. Carhart, 530 U.S. 914 (2000).
164. Homer v Evans, 517 US 620 (1996)
165. Lawrence v Texas, 539 US 558 (2003)

CHAPTER 12
166. VFW v Ken Salazar, US Secretary of the Interior (CV-11-284 US District Ct.E.D.C.Dof Ca) (2011)
167. See www.ca7.uscourts.gov/tmp/710JY5ZX.pdf
168. Edward Lutzer, When A Nation Forgets God: 7 Lessons we must learn from Nazi Germany, Moody Publishers, Chicago, IL, 2009
169. Jim Lovino, "Jesus Missing from Obama's Georgetown Speech," NBC Washington, April 17, 2009
170. Johanna Neuman, "Obama en Bush-era National Prayer Day Service at White House," Los Angeles Times, May 7, 2009
171. Barack Obama, "Remarks by the President at Iftar Dinner," The White House, September 1, 2009

172. Meredith Jessup, "Obama Continues to Omit 'Creator' From Declaration of Independence," The Blaze, October 19, 2010
173. Patrick Goodenough,"White House 'Strongly Objects' to Legislation Protecting Military Chaplains from Doing Same Sex Weddings or being Forced to Act Against Conscience," cnsnews.com, May 16, 2012
174. Courtesy Ronald Presidential Library—Simi Valley, California, by the National Archives and Records Administration.
175. R.J. Rushdoony, Law and Liberty (Fairfax, VA: Thorburn, 1971) p 33
176. Edward Lutzer, When a Nation Forgets God, Moody Press, Chicago, IL, 2009

EPILOGUE
177. ACLU of Tennessee v Hamilton County, (2002), 202 F Supp 2d 757 (E.D. Tenn. 2002)
178. ACLU of Kentucky v Grayson County (2002), WL 1558688 (W.D. Ky. May 13, 2002)
179. ACLU v City of Birmingham (1986), 791 F. Supp 1561 (6th Cir. 1986)
180. Wallace v Jeffree (1985),472 US 38, 43-44,n.22 (1985)
181. Draper v Logan County Public Library, 4403 f. supp 2d 608 (W.D. KY 2005)
182. Nichol v Arin Intermediate Unit 28, 268 F Supp.2d 536 (W.D. Pa 2003)
183. Peck v Baldwinsville Cent. Sch Dist (2005), 99-CV-1847 (N.D. N.Y. Aug.16, 2004)
184. Chandler v James (1997). CV 96-D-169-N. pp. 3-4, 6-7, 15 (M.D. Ala Oct.29, 1997
185. Stone v Graham (1980),449 US 39 (1980).
186. "Faith Talk: Important Info," National Foundation for the Blind, November 15, 2005 (at: http://www.ndbnet.org/pipermail/faith-talk/2003-November/0033354.html), Laurie Goodstein, "Discipling of Student is Defended," Washington Post, December 6, 1994..
187. Dana Blanton, "Courts Driving Religion Out of Public Life; Christianity Under Attack," Fox News.com, December 1, 2005.
188. Hamilton, Jay and Madison, p. 352, Federalist #65 by Alexander Hamilton.
189. Jefferson, Memoirs, Vol. IV, p 317, to Judge Spencer Roane on September, 1819

190. John Jay, The Correspondence and Public Papers of John Jay, Henry P. Johnston, editor (New York: G.P. Putnam's Sons, 1890) Vol. I, pp 163-164
191. Marlin Maddoux, Public Education Against America (New Kensington, Pa: Whitaker House, 2006), p 141-42
192. Kelly Shackleford, The Survey of Religious Hostility in America, Liberty Institute, 2001 West Plano Parkway, Suite 1600, Plano, TX 75075 (2012)

CHAPTER 13
193. Jerome Corsi, Bad Samaritans, The ACLU'S Relentless Campaign To Erase Faith from the Public Square, Thomas Nelson Inc., Publisher, Nashville, Tennessee, (2013)